2021年全国文化艺术职业院校和旅游职业院校
"学党史 迎百年"课程思政展示活动入选课程配套教材
吉林省高职院校精品在线开放课程配套教材
高等职业教育英语类课程新形态一体化教材

情景交际英语
了解中国
understanding China

主编 朱林莉

副主编 王锐 王卓 李幻宇

参编 单旭 林佳 刘沫 甘莹

主审 李娌

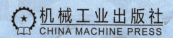

机械工业出版社
CHINA MACHINE PRESS

在"一带一路"沿线国家文化交融的时代背景下,本书立足于传播中华优秀传统文化,传递好中国声音,讲述好中国故事,展示好中国形象。

本书是吉林省高职院校精品在线开放课程配套教材。全书分为八个单元,分别是中国印象、中国记忆、自然景观、历史古迹、经典国粹、中国美食、中国节日、风土人情,共20节课。各节课分成七个部分,分别是热身活动、情景对话演练、主题阅读、课后练习、拓展阅读、参考译文和参考答案。

本书在超星学习通上有示范教学包"情景交际英语——了解中国(机工版)",提供教学微课、课件、情景动画等丰富的教学资源,凡使用本书的教师可通过超星学习通APP,一键引用示范教学包,开展混合式教学。

本书情景动画以二维码形式放在书中,读者只要用手机扫一扫书中二维码,即可随时观看学习。

本书还配有精美的教学课件,凡使用本书作为教材的教师可登录机械工业出版社教育服务网www.cmpedu.com下载。咨询电话:010-88379375。

图书在版编目(CIP)数据

情景交际英语:了解中国/朱林莉主编.
—北京:机械工业出版社,2021.5
高等职业教育英语类课程新形态一体化教材
ISBN 978-7-111-68284-4

Ⅰ.①情… Ⅱ.①朱… Ⅲ.①英语-高等职业教育-教材
Ⅳ.①H319.39

中国版本图书馆 CIP 数据核字(2021)第 097265 号

机械工业出版社(北京市百万庄大街22号 邮政编码100037)
策划编辑:杨晓昱　责任编辑:杨晓昱　徐梦然
责任校对:黄兴伟　版式设计:张文贵
封面设计:马精明　责任印制:常天培
固安县铭成印刷有限公司印刷
2021年8月第1版·第1次印刷
184mm×260mm·9.5印张·204千字
0001—1500册
标准书号:ISBN 978-7-111-68284-4
定价:36.00元

电话服务　　　　　　　网络服务
客服电话:010-88361066　机　工　官　网:www.cmpbook.com
　　　　　010-88379833　机　工　官　博:weibo.com/cmp1952
　　　　　010-68326294　金　书　网:www.golden-book.com
封底无防伪标均为盗版　机工教育服务网:www.cmpedu.com

前　言

《大学英语教学指南》对大学英语课程"人文性"的定位为："大学英语课程的重要任务之一是进行跨文化教育。语言是文化的载体，同时也是文化的组成部分，学生学习和掌握英语这一交流工具，除了学习、交流先进的科学技术或专业信息之外，还要了解国外的社会与文化，增进对不同文化的理解、对中外文化异同的意识，培养跨文化交际能力。人文性的核心是以人为本，弘扬人的价值，注重人的综合素质培养和全面发展。社会主义核心价值观应有机融入大学英语教学内容。因此，要充分挖掘大学英语课程丰富的人文内涵，实现工具性和人文性的有机统一。"

在"一带一路"沿线国家文化交融的时代背景下，本书立足于传播中华优秀传统文化，传递好中国声音，讲述好中国故事，展示好中国形象。

本书分为八个单元，分别是：中国印象、中国记忆、自然景观、历史古迹、经典国粹、中国美食、中国节日、风土人情，共 20 节课。每节课分成七个部分，各部分的功能如下：

第一部分为热身活动，是单元情景导入部分。使用文化主题关键词创设与各个单元主题相关的情景，将本单元的内容以关键词讨论等形式引出，增加课程的互动性和趣味性。

第二部分为情景对话演练，设置了国际交换生 Sam 和中国学生 Sally 的情景对话，在情景演练中设置了引导式提问练习，引发思考。练习中包括了重点单词、句型、句子结构以及情景表演。本部分是教学重点，要求学习者通过模仿、背诵、情景模拟演练等学习方法达到融会贯通的程度。

第三部分为主题阅读，进一步深化对单元主题的理解和掌握。

第四部分为课后练习，巩固本单元所学知识，帮助学生学以致用。

第五部分为拓展阅读，拓展相关知识。

第六部分为参考译文。

第七部分为参考答案。

本书是首批吉林省高职院校精品在线开放课程配套教材，也是 2021 年全国文化艺术职业院校和旅游职业院校"学党史　迎百年"课程思政展示活动入选课程配套教材。

本书将教材资源、课堂资源和教学资源三者融合。教学微课通过教师讲解与场景融入，直观形象地展示中国传统文化主题信息，引发思考；情景动画通过国际交换生 Sam 和中国学生 Sally 的对话，使学生融入情景之中，寓教于乐，动画配音由美籍专业人士录制，语音纯正，情景性强，便于模仿。

教学微课可以从超星学习通平台一键引用示范教学包。情景动画以二维码形式放在书中，读者只要用手机扫一扫书中二维码，即可随时观看学习。

本书配有精美的教学课件，凡使用本书作为教材的教师可登录机械工业出版社教育服务网 www.cmpedu.com 下载。咨询电话：010-88379375。

本书可供高职高专及以上水平的各专业的大学生使用，也可供中国传统文化爱好者自学，还可供旅游从业人员、民航从业人员作为中国传统文化培训材料使用。

本书在编写过程中承蒙机械工业出版社编辑以及同行们的大力支持，参阅了大量的相关资料，在此表示真诚的谢意。由于编者水平有限，书中难免有不足之处，敬请读者和业内专家多提宝贵意见。

编　者

情景动画二维码清单

名称	图形	名称	图形
1-1 The Four Great New Inventions 新四大发明		3-2 Jiuzhaigou 九寨沟	
1-2 Confucianism 儒家思想		4-1 The Great Wall 长城	
2-1 Seal Cutting 印章篆刻		4-2 The Forbidden City 紫禁城	
2-2 Chinese Shadow Puppetry 皮影戏		5-1 Calligraphy 书法	
3-1 The West Lake 西湖		5-2 Peking Opera 京剧	

（续）

名称	图形	名称	图形
5-3 Zhusuan 珠算		7-3 The Lantern Festival 元宵节	
6-1 Hot Pot 火锅		7-4 The Mid-Autumn Festival 中秋节	
6-2 Peking Duck 北京烤鸭		8-1 Chinese Paper-Cuts 剪纸	
7-1 The Spring Festival 春节		8-2 Chinese Kite 风筝	
7-2 The Dragon Boat Festival 端午节		8-3 Tai Chi 太极	

目 录

前　言
情景动画二维码清单

Unit I
The Impression of China
中国印象

Lesson 1　The Four Great New Inventions
　　　　　新四大发明　　　　　　　　　　// 002
Lesson 2　Confucianism　儒家思想　　　　// 008

Unit II
The Fading Memory
中国记忆

Lesson 1　Seal Cutting　印章篆刻　　　　　// 014
Lesson 2　Chinese Shadow Puppetry　皮影戏　// 021

Unit III
Natural Landscape
自然景观

Lesson 1　The West Lake　西湖　　　　　　// 030
Lesson 2　Jiuzhaigou　九寨沟　　　　　　　// 037

Unit IV
Historical Sites
历史古迹

Lesson 1　The Great Wall　长城　　　　　　// 046
Lesson 2　The Forbidden City　紫禁城　　　// 053

Unit V
Quintessence of Chinese Culture 经典国粹

Lesson 1	Calligraphy 书法	// 060
Lesson 2	Peking Opera 京剧	// 066
Lesson 3	Zhusuan 珠算	// 073

Unit VI
Chinese Cuisine 中国美食

| Lesson 1 | Hot Pot 火锅 | // 080 |
| Lesson 2 | Peking Duck 北京烤鸭 | // 087 |

Unit VII
Chinese Holidays 中国节日

Lesson 1	The Spring Festival 春节	// 096
Lesson 2	The Dragon Boat Festival 端午节	// 102
Lesson 3	The Lantern Festival 元宵节	// 109
Lesson 4	The Mid-Autumn Festival 中秋节	// 115

Unit VIII
Chinese Customs 风土人情

Lesson 1	Chinese Paper-Cuts 剪纸	// 124
Lesson 2	Chinese Kites 风筝	// 130
Lesson 3	Tai Chi 太极	// 136

Unit I
The Impression of China
中国印象

Lesson 1 The Four Great New Inventions
新四大发明

Warm-Up

Work in pairs. Learn the following words and phrases. Then answer the following questions.

1. Do you know what are the four great inventions in ancient China?
2. Can you list some technological innovations today?

Words and Expressions

Read the following words and expressions. Then try to memorize them.

innovation *n.* 创新	automatic *a.* 自动的；无意识的
manual *a.* 手控的；用手的	confirm *v.* 确认；确定

Useful Expressions

1. I haven't seen you in a few days. How are you?
2. These new inventions have made the daily life of the public more and more convenient.
3. You should scan the QR code on the bike with your phone.
4. You may need to confirm the amount and pay by your WeChat or Alipay.
5. I believe it promotes a low-carbon lifestyle as well.

Dialogue

Watch the animation, then practice the dialogue by reading it aloud with your partner. Read it through at least twice, and change your role each time.

(**Scene:** Sally is a college student in Cultural and Tourism School from China. Sam is an exchange student from America. In the classroom at campus, Sally and Sam are talking about the new inventions in the world.)

Sam: Hey, Sally. It's good to see you.
Sally: You too. I haven't seen you in a few days. How are you?

Lesson 1 The Four Great New Inventions 新四大发明

Sam: Not too bad. I'm busy with schoolwork. How about you?

Sally: I am working on a report about the Four Great New Inventions.

Sam: I know the Four Great Inventions of ancient China. I've never heard of the Four Great New Inventions.

Sally: It's a hot topic on the Internet.

Sam: Tell me about that.

Sally: Sure, the Four Great New Inventions are bike sharing, high speed rail, electronic payment and online shopping. Thanks to the technological innovations, these new inventions have made the daily life of the public more and more convenient.

Sam: Great. I would like to know how to use the shared bikes.

Sally: To get started, you have to have the shared bike application ready on your phone. When you get into the application, you'll see a map on the front page showing available bikes nearby. Follow the direction, and you are able to find your bike.

Sam: And then?

Sally: You should scan the QR code on the bike with your phone to unlock the bike. Then it is ready to go. The application will start the timer automatically.

Sam: How to lock the bike then?

Sally: When you reach the destination, you need to manually lock the bike.

Sam: That's great! And how do I pay?

Sally: The application will stop the timer and calculate the cost automatically. You may need to confirm the amount and pay by your WeChat or Alipay.

Sam: Wonderful! We can use it anywhere and anytime we want.

Sally: Yeah, we do not need to worry about traffic congestion.

Questions:

1. What are the Four Great New Inventions?
2. Can you briefly explain how to use shared bikes?

➡ Role-Play

Act it out according to the instructions.

A student from China: Sally

1. Greetings.
2. Sally tells him these technological innovations are convenient for our daily life.
3. Sally tells him how to use the shared bikes.

A student from America: Sam

1. Greetings.
2. To show curiosity about the Four Great New Inventions.
3. To ask some details about shared bikes.

Passage Reading

The Four Great Inventions refer to the four inventions in ancient China that had great influences on the world. They are papermaking, printing, gunpowder and compass. Papermaking and printing led to revolutionary progress in recording and transmitting information. The invention and spread of gunpowder changed the mode of war in the Middle Ages. And the compass greatly helped European navigators to explore new routes. The Four Great Inventions are symbols of advanced science and technology in ancient China and are of great significance in the development of Chinese and the world's civilizations.

Useful Words and Expressions:

gunpowder *n.* 火药	revolutionary *a.* 革命的
navigator *n.* 航海家	symbol *n.* 象征，符号
advanced science 先进科学	

Translation Tasks:

1. 四大发明是指中国古代对世界有巨大影响的四种发明。
2. 火药的发明和传播改变了中世纪的战争模式。
3. 指南针极大地帮助了欧洲航海家探索新航路。
4. Papermaking and printing led to revolutionary progress in recording and transmitting information.
5. The Four Great Inventions are of great significance in the development of Chinese and the world's civilizations.

Exercises

Ⅰ. *Match the following words and phrases, and write the corresponding letter for each item.*

1. convenient　　　_____　　a. 革命的
2. destination　　　_____　　b. 应用
3. congestion　　　_____　　c. 便利的

Lesson 1 The Four Great New Inventions 新四大发明

4. electronic payment _____   d. 意义
5. application _____   e. 拥堵
6. automatically _____   f. 方向
7. direction _____   g. 目的地
8. advanced science _____   h. 自动地
9. revolutionary _____   i. 先进科学
10. significance _____   j. 电子支付

II. Fill in the blanks according to the text.

1. If you want to use the shared bikes, you have to download _____ on your phone.
2. The Four Great New Inventions are _____.
3. Technological inventions can make everyday life _____.
4. _____ are the Four Great Inventions in ancient China.
5. The application can stop the timer and calculate the cost _____.

III. Translate the following sentences according to the dialogue.

1. Thanks to the technological innovations, these new inventions have made the daily life of the public more and more convenient.
2. The application will start the timer automatically.
3. You'll see a map on the front page showing available bikes nearby.
4. When you reach the destination, you need to manually lock the bike.
5. You may need to confirm the amount and pay by your WeChat or Alipay.

IV. Work in pairs and discuss the following questions.

1. Why are the shared bikes damaged by some people?
2. Do you think electronic payment is safe?

➡ Knowledge Expansion

The ancient Chinese invention of wooden movable-type printing is being preserved and developed in the village of Dongyuan, Wenzhou.

One-centimeter wooden cubes are arrayed in a jet-black rectangular frame. A reversed Chinese character is sculpted on each cube. Repeatedly smeared with ink for many years, these pale yellow matrices have been dyed nearly dark enough to match the ink itself. Once the matrices are inked, a high-quality Chinese art paper is placed on the top of them. The paper is then brushed and smoothed until the ink marks appear. Once the paper is removed, the page is printed with vertical, traditional Chinese characters. Assembling and binding such pages together produces a book.

Wang Chaohui, 60, inherited the traditional trade from his grandfather. In Dongyuan, there are around 20 technicians like Wang. Thanks to the strong cultural influence and large demand for genealogy, this technique has been successfully handed down from one generation to the next. Genealogy is an important concept in Wenzhou. Over the past decades, Wang has sculpted over 10,000 wooden movable-type cubes every year. He has also used nearly 100 engraving knives and over 7,000 sheets of art paper. Wang explained that genealogy generally consists of four or five volumes. They are revised and updated every 20 to 30 years, or as frequently as every 10 years in some areas. In terms of cost and operating efficiency, wooden movable-type printing is the best choice for these records. The only person who could "inherit" the technique from Wang is his 32-year-old son, Wang Jianxin. However, so far, Wang Jianxin has not demonstrated any special skill at the core technique of sculpting. Of the 20 technicians in Dongyuan who are able to work on genealogy revision, not a single one is below 50 years of age.

参考译文

课文阅读

四大发明是指中国古代对世界有巨大影响的四种发明,即造纸术、印刷术、火药和指南针。造纸术和印刷术使信息的记录和传播有了革命性的进步。火药的发明和传播改变了中世纪的战争模式。而指南针极大地帮助了欧洲航海家探索新航路。四大发明是中国古代先进科学和技术的象征,在中国和世界文明发展中都有着重要的意义。

扩展阅读

古老的中国发明木制活字印刷术在温州东源村得以存续及发展。

边长为一厘米的木制小方块被整齐排列,放到一个乌黑的矩形框架中。一个个方向颠倒的汉字被雕刻在每个小方块上。刻有汉字的小方块可以被重复地染墨很多年,这些浅黄色的矩阵已几乎被染至黑色,足以与墨色相媲美。一旦这些字块被染色,就会将高质量的中国美术纸覆于其上。之后,用刷子在纸上来回刷动以使纸张平滑,直到沾有墨水的小方块清晰地印出汉字。一旦拿起纸张,纸上就会出现方向正确的印刷汉字。之后,将印刷好的纸张整合并装订成书。

60岁的王朝晖是从其祖父处继承的印刷技术。在东源村,与王先生从事相同职业的技术人员约有20个。多亏了强有力的文化影响和对家谱的大量需求,此项技术得以世代传承下来。家谱在温州是一个重要的概念。过去的数十年间,王先生每年都雕刻超过10,000

Lesson 1　The Four Great New Inventions　新四大发明

个木制活字印刷字块。他也曾经使用过大约100把刻刀和7,000多张纸。王先生抱怨道，家谱通常都包含4卷至5卷内容。每20年到30年，都需对这些族谱进行修订和更新，一些地方更是每10年就对某些方面的内容进行修订和更新。考虑成本和经营的有效性，木制活字印刷是制作这些记录的最好选择。唯一可以继承此项技艺的人是王先生32岁的儿子王建新。然而，截至目前，王建新对于雕刻的核心技术都没有展现出任何特殊天赋。并且，在东源镇的这20位技术人员中，可以进行家谱修订的人没有一个是年龄小于50岁的。

参考答案

Exercises

Ⅰ．1—5　c g e j b　　6—10　h f i a d

Ⅱ．1. an application

2. bike sharing, high speed rail, electronic payment and online shopping

3. convenient

4. Papermaking, printing, gunpowder and compass

5. automatically

Ⅲ．1. 多亏这些技术革新，这些新发明让公众的日常生活变得越来越方便。

2. 应用程序会自动开始计时。

3. 你会在首页看到一张地图，显示附近可用的共享单车。

4. 当你到达目的地时，你需要手动给它上锁。

5. 你需要确认付款金额，然后用微信或支付宝支付就可以了。

Ⅳ．Omitted

Lesson 2　Confucianism　儒家思想

Warm-Up

Work in pairs. Learn the following words and phrases. Then answer the following questions.

1. Can you recite a passage of *the Analects of Confucius*?
2. Please briefly introduce Confucius.

➡ Words and Expressions

Read the following words and expressions. Then try to memorize them.

philosophy *n.* 哲学；哲理；人生观	classical *a.* 经典的；古典的
profound *a.* 意义深远的；渊博的	effect *n.* 影响；效果；作用
at a loss 不知所措；茫然	

➡ Useful Expressions

1. I am completely at a loss while reading classical Chinese.
2. It is said that Confucius was not a good-looking guy.
3. Can you give me a brief introduction?
4. Confucius is ranked at the top in "the world's top ten cultural celebrities".
5. Confucianism, led by him, has exerted profound influence on Chinese people.

➡ Dialogue

Watch the animation, then practice the dialogue by reading it aloud with your partner. Read it through at least twice, and change your role each time.

(**Scene:** Sally is a college student in Cultural and Tourism School from China. Sam is an exchange student from America. In the classroom at campus, Sam is reading some classical Chinese books.)

Sam: I am very interested in ancient Chinese philosophy, but I am completely at a loss while reading classical Chinese.

Sally: I won't blame you. Classical Chinese is difficult, sometimes even Chinese people are not able to completely understand it.

Sam: Can you give me a brief introduction?

Sally: Sure! Confucianism has influenced Chinese people for thousands of years and occupies an important position in the history of Chinese thought.

Sam: Why?

Sally: Confucius is ranked at the top in "the world's top ten cultural celebrities". Confucianism, led by him, has exerted profound influence on Chinese people. To understand China, you must understand Confucianism; to understand Confucianism, you should get to know Confucius.

Sam: Do you have photos of Confucius?

Sally: It is said that Confucius was not a good-looking guy. The middle of his head is low while the other part is high. And he was about 1.9 meters tall. So, Confucius is probably like this…

Sam: Oh, that's Confucius!

Sally: If you want to know more about Confucius, I recommend you to watch the film *Confucius*.

Sam: Thanks a lot.

Questions:

1. Does Confucius have a good looking?
2. Why does Confucianism have a deep influence on the people in China?

➡ Role-Play

Act it out according to the instructions.

A student from China: Sally

1. Greetings.
2. Sally gives a brief introduction of Confucius and Confucianism.
3. Sally shows him a photo of Confucius.

A student from America: Sam

1. Greetings.
2. Sam is very confused about classical Chinese.
3. Sam is curious about the looking of Confucius.

Passage Reading

Confucianism is the largest Chinese school of thought, and was the mainstream consciousness of the ancient China. Confucianism had been one of the ruling doctrines of the feudal ruling class since the Han Dynasty. The core of Confucianism is actually a kind of humanism. It advocates self-cultivation, and believes that human beings are teachable and improvable. A grand goal of Confucianism is to achieve a harmonious society in which each individual plays his or her part well, and maintains a good relationship with others.

Useful Words and Expressions:

Confucianism *n.* 儒家思想	mainstream *n.* 主流
consciousness *n.* 意识	doctrine *n.* 主义，学说
feudal *a.* 封建制度的	humanism *n.* 人道主义
feudal ruling class 封建统治阶级	

Translation Tasks:

1. 儒家思想是中国古代的主流意识。
2. 儒家思想的核心其实是一种人道主义。
3. 在这样的一个社会中，每个人都能扮演好自己的角色。
4. Confucianism had been one of the ruling doctrines of the feudal ruling class since the Han Dynasty.
5. It advocates self-cultivation, and believes that human beings are teachable and improvable.
6. A grand goal of Confucianism is to achieve a harmonious society.

Exercises

I. *Match the following words and phrases, and write the corresponding letter for each item.*

1. exert　　　　　　　_____　　a. 修养
2. Confucianism　　　_____　　b. 名人
3. blame　　　　　　 _____　　c. 文言文
4. classical Chinese　 _____　　d. 学说
5. celebrity　　　　　 _____　　e. 施加
6. harmonious　　　　_____　　f. 提倡
7. advocate　　　　　_____　　g. 责备

8. consciousness　　　　_____　　　h. 和谐的
9. self-cultivation　　　　_____　　　i. 儒家思想
10. doctrine　　　　　　　_____　　　j. 意识

Ⅱ. *Fill in the blanks according to the text.*

1. Confucianism believes that _____.
2. _____ is the core of Confucianism.
3. When Sam is reading classical Chinese, he is _____.
4. If you want to get to know Chinese culture, you have to _____.
5. The great aim of Confucianism is to _____.

Ⅲ. *Translate the following sentences according to the dialogue.*

1. Confucianism has influenced Chinese people for thousands of years and occupies an important position in the history of Chinese thought.
2. It is said that Confucius was not a good-looking guy.
3. Confucius is ranked at the top in "the world's top ten cultural celebrities".
4. To understand China, you must understand Confucianism; to understand Confucianism, you should get to know Confucius.
5. I am very interested in ancient Chinese philosophy, but I am completely at a loss while reading classical Chinese.

Ⅳ. *Work in pairs and discuss the following questions.*

1. How do you think about the educational thoughts of Confucius?
2. Do you think a college education can change a person's life?

Knowledge Expansion

Confucius is one of the most famous sages of China. More than any other single man, he, through his followers, produced the principle basis of the Chinese tradition of ethics and political theory that had deeply influenced Chinese society and culture. Over the centuries, this influence had spread also to Republic of Korea, Japan and other countries.

参考译文

课文阅读

儒家思想是中国古代最大的思想流派，也是中国古代的主流意识。自汉代以来，儒家思想就是封建统治阶级的指导思想之一。儒家思想的核心其实是一种人道主义。它提倡自我修养，认为人是可教化的、可完善的。儒家思想的一个宏大的目标就是实现"大同社会"，在这样的一个社会中，每个人都能扮演好自己的角色，并与他人维持良好的关系。

扩展阅读

孔子是中国最知名的圣人之一。相比其他人，孔子和他的追随者奠定了中国传统的道德观和政治理论的原则依据，对中国社会和文化产生了深远的影响。几个世纪以来，这种影响还传播到韩国、日本等国家。

参考答案

Exercises

Ⅰ. 1—5　e i g c b　　6—10　h f j a d

Ⅱ. 1. human beings are teachable and improvable

2. Humanism

3. at a loss

4. understand Confucianism

5. achieve harmonious society

Ⅲ. 1. 儒家思想影响了中华民族几千年，在中国思想史上占有重要地位。

2. 据说孔子长得并不好看。

3. 孔子被评为"中国十大文化名人"之首。

4. 要想了解中国，就必须了解儒家思想；要了解儒家思想，就得了解孔子这个人。

5. 虽然我对中国古代哲学很感兴趣，但每当我阅读文言文的时候完全不知所措。

Ⅳ. Omitted

Unit II
The Fading Memory

中国记忆

Lesson 1　Seal Cutting　印章篆刻

Warm-Up

Work in pairs. Learn the following words and phrases. Then answer the following questions.

1. What is the official logo of the 2008 Beijing Olympics inspired by?
2. What are the ancient Chinese seals used for?
3. What were the seals for emperors called?

➡ Words and Expressions

Read the following words and expressions. Then try to memorize them.

inspire *v.* 赋予灵感；启发	carve *v.* 雕刻
calligraphy *n.* 书法	vacation *n.* 假期
unique *a.* 独一无二的	official logo 官方标识
trace back 追溯	

➡ Useful Expressions

1. It was an awesome experience.
2. The history of the Chinese seals could be traced back some 3,700 years ago.
3. It sounds great.
4. Seals started to gain popularity among scholars and officials.
5. Seals combine several art forms including calligraphy, sculpture, painting and designing.
6. Xis were only allowed to describe the seals for the emperors.

➡ Dialogue

Watch the animation, then practice the dialogue by reading it aloud with your partner. Read it through at least twice, and change your role each time.

(**Scene:** Sally is a college student in Cultural and Tourism School from China. Sam is an

Lesson 1　Seal Cutting　印章篆刻

exchange student from America. They are talking about the seal making activity Sally participated in her summer vacation.)

Sally: Wow, we had a great time on vacation.

Sam: Yeah, Lia told me that you went to a really cool place.

Sally: Yeah, it was an awesome experience.

Sam: Tell me more.

Sally: Well, we spent lots of time in the Xiling Seal Engravers' Society. We were happy because we had wonderful activities of seal making.

Sam: Where is it?

Sally: It is located at western Gushan Hill by the West Lake scenic area.

Sam: What about the seal making activity?

Sally: Em, it was so cool! The instructor taught us how to make a personal seal with our names in Chinese characters.

Sam: It sounds great! Tell me something about Chinese seals.

Sally: Seal cutting incorporates the skills of calligraphy and carving.

Sam: Is it unique to China?

Sally: Yeah, it is several thousand years old. The finest seals have become collectors' items.

Sam: I heard the inspiration for the design of the emblem for the 2008 Beijing Olympics Games came from seal cutting.

Sally: That's right.

Sam: Do you have your personal seal?

Sally: Of course. Take a look.

Sam: Wow! It's awesome.

Sally: Do you want your own seal?

Sam: Yeah, I can't wait.

Questions:

1. Where is Xiling located at?
2. What skills does seal making incorporate?
3. Where was seal originated from?
4. What is the purpose of a seal?
5. What are Chinese seals made of?

Role-Play

Act it out according to the instructions.

A student in China: Sally

1. Greets Sam in a casual and friendly way.
2. Gives Sam a brief introduction on the Chinese Seals.
3. Shows Sam her personal seal.

A student from America: Sam

1. Greets Sally in a casual and friendly way.
2. Asks about the Chinese seals.
3. Gives comments on Sally's seal.

Passage Reading

History behind Chinese Seals

The seal was first created in 221 BC. After the first emperor of China, Qin Shi Huang, conquered the six Warring States and unified China, he ordered his first imperial seal to be carved using beautiful white jade. The imperial seal was called the "Xi" and was only used by those in power.

The emperors who followed used an imperial seal, but the number of seals changed depending on the dynasty and who was in power.

It wasn't until the Ming (1368—1644) and Qing (1636—1911) Dynasties that the seal's usage moved from the imperial to the personal, due to the expansion of the feudal arts. Artists began using a stylized seal carving of their name to mark ownership of their works. Individuals also began using a personalized stamp for important documents. These non-official stamps were called "Yin".

Useful Words and Expressions:

conquer *v.* 占领；征服	unify *v.* 整合；统一
jade *n.* 玉；翡翠	imperial *a.* 帝国的；皇帝的
feudal *a.* 封建的	ownership *n.* 所有权

Translation Tasks:

1. 皇帝的印章被称为玺。

Lesson 1　Seal Cutting　印章篆刻

2. 印章由美丽的白玉雕刻而成。

3. 秦始皇征服了六国，统一了中国。

4. The seal's usage moved from the imperial to the personal, due to the expansion of the feudal arts.

5. Artists began using a stylized seal carving of their name to mark ownership of their works.

6. Individuals also began using a personalized stamp for important documents.

➡ Exercises

Ⅰ. *Match the following words and phrases, and write the corresponding letter for each item.*

1. stylized　　　_____　　a. 所有权
2. personalized　_____　　b. 皇帝的
3. expansion　　_____　　c. 官方的
4. ownership　　_____　　d. 风格化的
5. official　　　_____　　e. 定制的
6. imperial　　　_____　　f. 扩张

Ⅱ. *Fill in the blanks according to the text.*

1. The first emperor of China, _____, conquered the six Warring States and unified China.

2. The first imperial seal was carved using _____.

3. The seal's usage moved from the _____ to the _____.

4. The seal was first created in _____ .

5. These non-official stamps were called _____ .

Ⅲ. *Translate the following sentences according to the dialogue.*

1. It was an awesome experience.

2. Seal cutting incorporates the skills of calligraphy and carving.

3. The finest seals have become collectors' items.

4. We spent lots of time in the Xiling Seal Engravers' Society.

5. 我们参加了很棒的印章制作活动。

6. 老师教我们怎么做带有自己名字的印章。

7. 2008 北京奥运会标识的设计灵感来自于印章雕刻。

8. 中国印章的历史可以追溯到 3,700 年前。

IV. *Work in pairs and discuss the following questions.*

1. How are seals used today?
2. Does a seal carver need to be a good Chinese calligrapher?

Knowledge Expansion

Types of Seals for Chinese Art Works

Name Seals

This is the seal with your name on it. It tells people who made this painting or calligraphy. Since in China different names are used for the same person, and in different occasions of your art work different names need to be used, there is also a complicated system to make different names seals and use them for different occasions. Therefore, strictly speaking, one person normally has several name seals for different occasions.

Nowadays, people are not as strict as ancient Chinese people on using name seals. However, it is still a common practice to prepare two name seals: one is carved in Yin and the other in Yang. One piece of art work needs a pair of such seals. Both should have similar size. Regarding the shape of the name seals, Zhang Daqian believed that name seals should be best in square shape; round shape is also acceptable. Except square and rounds shapes, all other shapes should not be used for name seals.

Decoration Seals

"Xian" literally means leisure. Although its name sounds unimportant, it is an important contributor to the whole artistic effect of the painting. This type of seal is used strictly for several specific places of the art work, for example, the starting point of the painting and calligraphy, the edge of the art work, the middle of the art work, etc. Therefore, such decoration seals are also referred to as "location seal" ("Bu Ju Zhang"). "Bu Ju" means to locate, and Zhang means seal.

Collector's Seals

This is a special type of seal used by collectors. This tradition started in Tang Dynasty. When a collector gets a valuable piece of art work, for example, painting, calligraphy, or book, he would use his collector's seal to stamp on the art work. However, you need to be careful with where you stamp the seal. The principle is not to destroy the original painting balance. However, this principle is very easy to be broken since every collector wants to leave a stamp on the art work. *Lanting Xu* is an example of using collector's seals.

参考译文

课文阅读

印章背后的历史

印章最早诞生于公元前221年。中国第一任皇帝秦始皇攻克了六国并统一了中国后，下令用美丽的白玉来雕刻他的第一枚印章。皇帝的印章被称为玺，只能被皇帝所用。

后代皇帝也延续使用印章，但是不同的朝代，不同的皇帝所用的印章数量并不相同。

由于封建艺术的发展，直到明清，印章才可为平民所用。艺术家用个性鲜明的姓名印章去标注他们的著作权。人们也用印章来标注重要文件。这些非官方的印章被称为印。

扩展阅读

姓名章

姓名章是一种刻有个人名字的印章，用来标注绘画和书法作品。因为在中国，一个人可能使用不同的名字，在不同场合下，艺术作品也需要使用不同的姓名章。因此，存在一个复杂的系统用以制作不同的姓名章，并在不同场合使用它们。严格来说，一个人通常在不同场合具有多个姓名章。

如今，人们对于姓名章的使用要求不如古代人严格。但是，准备两个姓名章仍然是一种普遍的做法：一种叫阴刻，另一种叫阳刻。一件艺术品需要一对这样的印章。两者应具有相似的大小。关于印章的形状，张大千认为，印章最好是正方形的，圆形是可以接受的。除正方形和圆形外，其他所有形状均不应用于姓名章。

闲章

"闲"的字面意思是休闲。尽管它的名字听起来并不重要，但它对一幅画整体的艺术效果具有重要意义。这种类型的印章严格用于艺术品的几个特定位置，如绘画和书法作品的起点、艺术品的边缘、艺术品的中间等。因此，闲章也被称为"布局章"。"布局"表示定位，"章"表示印章。

鉴赏章

这是收藏家所使用的特殊类型的印章。这一传统始于唐代。当收藏家拿到一件有价值的艺术品时，如绘画、书法或书籍作品，他会用收藏家的印章在艺术品上盖章。但是，在加盖印章时需要小心。原则是不破坏原始绘画作品的平衡。但是，这个原则很难坚持，因为每个收藏家都希望在艺术品上留下印记。《兰亭序》就是一个使用了鉴赏章的例子。

参考答案

Exercises

Ⅰ. 1—6 d e f a c b

Ⅱ. 1. Qin Shi Huang

2. white jade

3. imperial; personal

4. 221 BC

5. Yin

Ⅲ. 1. 这是一次很棒的体验。

2. 印章篆刻融合了书法创作和雕刻艺术。

3. 最珍贵的印章成了鉴赏章。

4. 我们在西泠印章社团玩了很久。

5. We had wonderful activities of seal making.

6. The instructor taught us how to make a personal seal with my name in Chinese characters.

7. The inspiration for the design of the emblem for the 2008 Beijing Olympics Games came from seal cutting.

8. The history of which could be traced back some 3,700 years ago.

Ⅳ. Omitted

Lesson 2 Chinese Shadow Puppetry 皮影戏

Warm-Up

Work in pairs. Learn the following words and phrases. Then answer the following questions.

1. Have you ever seen Chinese shadow puppetry? Do you enjoy it?
2. What are those puppets made of?
3. How does a shadow puppet work?

➡ Words and Expressions

Read the following words and expressions. Then try to memorize them.

rod *n.* 杆，竿，棒	manipulate *v.* 操纵，控制
translucent *a.* 半透明的	storytelling *n.* 讲故事
troupe *n.* 剧团，戏班子，表演队	fanciful *a.* 空想的；想象的
joint *n.* 关节	accompanied by 伴随着
bring forth something 产生；发表	

➡ Useful Expressions

1. Shadow puppets are figures that are placed between a light and a screen.
2. An experienced puppeteer can make figures appear to walk, talk, fight and dance.
3. A complicated show would be staged by a troupe of seven to nine artists.
4. It could take as many as 24 steps and more than 3,000 cuts to produce a single figure.
5. It was also suitable for performing in military camps and remote villages.
6. Shadow puppetry is widely scattered across China, especially in rural areas.

➡ Dialogue

Watch the animation, then practice the dialogue by reading it aloud with your partner. Read it through at least twice, and change your role each time.

(**Scene:** Sally is a college student in Cultural and Tourism School from China. Sam is an exchange student from America. In the theatre, they are watching Chinese shadow plays. Sally is giving Sam a brief introduction on Chinese shadow puppetry.)

Sam: What's going on behind the screen?

Sally: A special performance.

Sam: What performance is it?

Sally: It's called the shadow puppetry, a world's intangible cultural heritage.

Sam: Tell me more about that.

Sally: The shadow puppetry is also called shadow play, an ancient form of entertainment.

Sam: Look, it was quite a lot of fun.

Sally: Yeah, really great! The body parts of the puppets are separately cut out and joined together. They may have up to 24 movable joints. Puppeteers hold them with rods linked to their most important joints during the performances, so that the puppets could be presented as "moving images" on the screens. The experienced puppeteers were able to manipulate five rods on one puppet with only one hand, so that a puppet could be as vivid as a living creature.

Sam: No wonder Chinese shadow puppetry is also dubbed as the "forefather of the films". I cannot wait to try a shadow puppetry dance.

Questions:

1. What type of show are they watching?
2. How many moveable joints can a puppet have?
3. How do puppeteers manipulate puppets?
4. Is Chinese shadow puppetry one of the origins of modern movie?

Role-Play

Act it out according to the instructions.

A student in China: Sally

1. Greets Sam in a casual way.
2. Gives Sam some introduction on Chinese shadow puppetry.
3. Answers questions from Sam.

A student from America: Sam

1. Greets Sally in a casual way.
2. Asks about Chinese shadow puppetry.
3. Asks how a puppeteer plays the puppet.

Lesson 2　Chinese Shadow Puppetry　皮影戏

Passage Reading

Chinese shadow puppetry, or shadow play, is probably one of the most ancient arts using light and shadow, thousands of years before its much more popular successor, the film.

However, unlike the film, which now enjoys a global market worth billions of US dollars and various glamorous awards and festivals, shadow puppetry has been fading from the spotlight.

In recent years, local artists and troupes across China have been exploring ways to revive the ancient art form and to pass it on to the next generation. Their effort has garnered encouragement and support from the Chinese government, which is devoted to national rejuvenation, including that of the country's traditional culture.

In 2011, Chinese shadow puppetry was added to UNESCO's Intangible Cultural Heritage list, thus injecting new vitality into the ancient art form.

Although it is still far from regaining its old glory, the ancient art form has found its value elsewhere.

Useful Words and Expressions:

successor *n.* 接替者；继任者	glamorous *a.* 有魅力的；令人向往的
fade *v.* （使）褪色；（使）变暗；（使）衰弱	revive *v.* （使）苏醒；（使）复原；（使）复兴
garner *v.* 收集，积累，获得	vitality *n.* 生命力；活力

Translation Tasks:

1. 皮影戏是最早利用光与影的艺术形式之一。
2. 皮影戏已逐渐淡出聚光灯。
3. 中国本土艺术家一直在寻找途径来复兴这种古老的艺术形式。
4. 他们的努力得到了中国政府的鼓励与支持。
5. The film now enjoys a global market worth billions of US dollars and various glamorous awards and festivals.
6. China is devoted to national rejuvenation, including that of the country's traditional culture.
7. In 2011, Chinese shadow puppetry was added to UNESCO's Intangible Cultural Heritage list, thus injecting new vitality into the ancient art form.
8. Although it is still far from regaining its old glory, the ancient art form has found its value elsewhere.

Exercises

I. Match the following words and phrases, and write the corresponding letter for each item.

1. revive   _____   a. 探索
2. regain   _____   b. 复兴
3. fade   _____   c. 褪色
4. garner   _____   d. 奉献
5. explore   _____   e. 收集
6. devote   _____   f. 恢复

II. Fill in the blanks according to the text.

1. Chinese shadow puppetry is one of the most ancient arts using _____ and _____.
2. Shadow puppetry has been _____ from the spotlight.
3. Their effort has garnered _____ and _____ from the Chinese government.
4. China is devoted to national rejuvenation, including that of the country's _____.
5. Chinese shadow puppetry is still far from _____.

III. Translate the following sentences according to the dialogue.

1. What's going on behind the screen?
2. The shadow puppetry is an ancient form of entertainment.
3. It was quite a lot of fun.
4. The body parts of the puppets are separately cut out and joined together.
5. 人偶有多达 24 个关节。
6. 表演者通过一根连接重要关节的杆子来操纵人偶。
7. 表演者可以单手操作五根杆。
8. 人偶像真人一样活灵活现。

IV. Work in pairs and discuss the following questions.

1. What country did shadow puppetry originate from?
2. How does a puppeteer play the puppet?

Knowledge Expansion

History

Shadow puppetry has a history of over 2,000 years, first originating during the Han

Dynasty (206 BC—220 AD). It is said that when one of the concubines of Emperor Wu died, he became inconsolable and was completely devastated. He even ignored the affairs of state and instead ordered his court officers to bring his beloved back to life. To satisfy his royal highness, they had the idea to recreate the shape of the concubine using donkey leather. Her joints were animated using 11 separate pieces of leather, and her beauty was recharged with painted clothes. Using an oil lamp, they made her shadow move, bringing her back to life. After seeing the shadow puppetry, Emperor Wu and his heart began to recover. This love story is recorded in the book titled, "The History of the Han Dynasty".

During the Song Dynasty, shadow plays became particularly popular. By the time of the Ming Dynasty, there were 40 to 50 shadow puppetry troupes in Beijing alone. In the late 13th century, in the reign of the Yuan Dynasty, the puppetry became a source of entertainment and recreation in the barracks of the Mongolian troops. As the Mongols swept across the continent and conquered Asia, they spread the popularity of shadow puppetry to distant countries such as Persia (Iran), Arabia, Turkey, and various Southeast Asian countries.

Evolution

There is even an iconic old ballad from the Shaanxi Province that describes what shadow play is:

Folk Shadow Play

Speaking behind paper partition screens,

Expressing variable feelings by shadows,

One shadow play actor can tell thousands of years of stories,

Both hands can operate millions of soldiers.

In recent years throughout many areas of China, certain types of plays and the art of shadow performance are near extinction. As the generations modernize, the old traditions begin to fade into history. Fortunately, however, shadow puppetry is alive and well-preserved especially in Huanxian County in northwest Gansu Province where there are still more than 90 active shadow puppetry groups, all of which are made up of local farmers. In 2003 this art form was named one of the first 10 key preserved intangible cultural heritages in China. The county is the birthplace of the Daoqing style of shadow puppetries, a classic and easy-to-understand style.

Daoqing plays involve only a single performer who manipulates all of the characters and impressively conducts the orchestra at the same time. Shi Chenglin, a famous artist from Huanxian County, has performed plays in more than 10 countries including Italy, Canada and the United States. Since 2005, the Huanxian County Shadow Puppetry Troupe has staged more than 50 Daoqing shadow puppetries in over 20 cities worldwide. In Italy, the popularity of the performances soared and audience members swarmed to the stage following the performance, eager to find out what happened behind the screen. Overall, the shows have sparked strong and wide interest among European audiences, winning the traditional storytelling and art form many fans.

参考译文

课文阅读

中国皮影戏很可能是最早运用光与影的艺术形式之一。皮影戏比它的继任者电影要早出现几千年。

但是，今天的电影已经是一个在全球市场上达数十亿美元的产业，并且赢得无数的赞誉和大奖。不同于电影，皮影戏逐渐地淡出了聚光灯。

近年来，一些中国本土的艺术家和表演团正在探索复兴皮影戏的路径，让皮影戏一代代传承下去。他们的努力得到了中国政府的大力支持。中国正在致力于民族复兴，其中当然包括了复兴中国传统文化。

2011年，皮影戏被联合国教科文组织列为非物质文化遗产，这为这种古老的艺术注入了新的活力。

尽管它还远未恢复昔日的辉煌，但这种古老的艺术形式在别处找到了它的价值。

扩展阅读

历史

皮影戏有2000多年的历史，最早起源于汉代（公元前206—公元220年）。据说，汉武帝的一个爱妃李夫人死于疾病，汉武帝思念心切，神情恍惚，终日不理朝政，他命令大臣们让逝者复活。大臣们用11块驴皮按照这个爱妃生前的模样做了个傀儡，关节可以灵活动起来，并且画出了华丽的衣服，在油灯下观看时栩栩如生，仿佛让她重生一般。在观看皮影戏之后汉武帝得以恢复。这个爱情故事在《汉书》里有记载。

在宋代，皮影戏开始盛行。到明朝，北京一带的皮影戏班达四五十家。13世纪末，皮影戏成为元代蒙古兵营里一种娱乐表演项目。随着蒙古人征服亚洲，皮影戏被随军带到波斯（伊朗）、阿拉伯、土耳其等国。后来，又在东南亚各国流传开来。

演变

有一首来自陕西省的传统民谣，描述了什么是皮影戏：

民间皮影戏，

Lesson 2　Chinese Shadow Puppetry　皮影戏

在纸隔板后面说话，

用阴影表达变幻莫测的情感。

一口道尽千古事，

双手挥舞百万兵。

近年来，中国许多地区的戏剧和皮影表演艺术正濒临灭绝。随着现代化进程的推进，古老的传统开始逐渐淡出历史。幸运的是，在甘肃西北的环县，皮影木偶技艺还迸发着蓬勃生机，那里还有90多个活跃的皮影剧团，由当地农民组成。2003年，皮影艺术形式被评为全国首批10项重点保护非物质文化遗产之一。该县是道情皮影戏的发源地，风格经典而通俗易懂。

道情皮影戏由一个表演者操纵所有的影偶，同时要兼顾声效。环县著名艺术家史呈林曾在意大利、加拿大、美国等10多个国家演出。2005年以来，环县皮影剧团在全球20多个城市演出了50多部道情皮影戏。在意大利，演出人气飙升，观众们在演出结束后蜂拥上台，急切地想知道银幕后面发生了什么。总之，这些节目在欧洲观众中引发了强烈而广泛的兴趣，为中国传统故事和艺术形式赢得了许多海外粉丝。

参考答案

Exercises

Ⅰ. 1—6　b f c e a d

Ⅱ. 1. light; shadow

　　2. fading

　　3. encouragement; support

　　4. traditional culture

　　5. regaining its old glory

Ⅲ. 1. 屏幕后面发生了什么？

　　2. 皮影戏是一种古老的娱乐形式。

　　3. 它非常有趣。

　　4. 人偶身体的各个部分被分开切割并连接在一起。

　　5. The puppets may have up to 24 movable joints.

　　6. Puppeteers hold them with rods linked to their most important joints during the performances.

　　7. The experienced puppeteers were able to manipulate five rods on one puppet with only one hand.

　　8. A puppet could be as vivid as a living creature.

Ⅳ. Omitted

Unit III
Natural Landscape
自然景观

Lesson 1　The West Lake　西湖

Warm-Up

Work in pairs. Learn the following words and phrases. Then answer the following questions.

1. Have you been to the West Lake? How do you feel?
2. If you work as a volunteer, how can you introduce Chinese culture to foreigners?

➡ Words and Expressions

Read the following words and expressions. Then try to memorize them.

allocate *v.* 分配	award *v.* 把（某物）授予（某人）；把（合同、佣金）给（人、组织）
certificate *n.* 证书；文凭，合格证书；电影放映许可证	contemporary *adj.* 发生（属）于同时期的；当代的
heritage *n.* 遗产；传统；继承物；继承权	recruiting *v.* 招募；聘请（recruit 的-ing 形式）
scenic *a.* 风景优美的	subsidy *n.* 补贴
volunteer *n.* 志愿者	the Broken Bridge 断桥

➡ Useful Expressions

1. Here comes the opportunity!
2. We are recruiting international volunteers to work at the West Lake.
3. Sounds cool!
4. All we want is your passion to work at the West Lake, and to learn about the Chinese culture.
5. You can simply scan the following QR code to sign up.

➡ Dialogue

Watch the animation, then practice the dialogue by reading it aloud with your partner. Read it through at least twice, and change your role each time.

Lesson 1　The West Lake　西湖

(**Scene:** Sally is a college student in Cultural and Tourism School from China. Sam is an exchange student from America. They are talking about what they are going to do at weekends.)

Sally: Hi Sam, do you have any idea to do something during the weekends?

Sam: No, I have absolutely no idea of what to do.

Sally: Well, here comes the opportunity! We are recruiting international volunteers to work at the West Lake.

Sam: Sounds cool!

Sally: Moreover, we are recruiting a long-term volunteers service team!

Sam: What services do we need to provide?

Sally: Volunteers will need to provide assistance, information on cultural, historical, and contemporary heritage, and translations to the tourists. Volunteers may be allocated to provide services at popular scenic spots such as the Broken Bridge.

Sam: Any requirements?

Sally: All we want is your passion to work at the West Lake, and to learn about the Chinese culture.

Sam: Any benefits?

Sally: Yeah, we provide necessary pre-job training, lunches, and certain transportation subsidies. A volunteer service hours certificate will be awarded at the end of your service.

Sam: That sounds great! How to apply then?

Sally: You can simply scan the following QR code to sign up.

Questions:

1. Do the volunteers have salaries? How are they paid?
2. What do they need to do when providing volunteering service?

 Role-Play

Act it out according to the instructions.

A student from China: Sally

1. Greetings.
2. Sally has been doing volunteering programs.
3. Sally suggests that he can take part in the international volunteer service.

A student from America: Sam

1. Greetings.
2. Sam doesn't know what to do at weekends.
3. Sam gets some advice from Sally.

Passage Reading

The West Lake, located in the western area of Hangzhou's center, is one of the top three lakes in the regions south of the Yangtze River. Because of it, Hangzhou has been acclaimed as a "heaven on earth" since ancient times. The West Lake is like a shining pearl inlaid on the vast land, and is renowned for its beautiful scenery, well-known historical sites, brilliant culture, and plentiful local specialties. The literary giant Su Shi in Song Dynasty left a timeless poetic masterpiece through the ages there: The West Lake is like the beauty Xi Shi, who is always charming with either light or heavy make-up (rainy or shiny). The Legend of the White Snake also brings the West Lake an air of mystery.

Useful Words and Expressions:

region *n.* 地区	pearl *n.* 珍珠
scenery *n.* 风景	masterpiece *n.* 杰作
charming *a.* 迷人的	

Translation Tasks:

1. 西湖是江南三大名湖之一。
2. 西湖就像镶嵌在广袤大地上的一颗璀璨的明珠。
3. 西湖以其秀丽的风景、著名的古迹、灿烂的文化和丰富的特产而闻名。
4. The Legend of the White Snake also brings the West Lake an air of mystery.
5. The West Lake is like the beauty Xi Shi, who is always charming with either light or heavy make-up.

Exercises

I. *Match the following words and phrases, and write the corresponding letter for each item.*

1. recruit　　　　＿＿＿＿＿　　a. 杰作
2. transportation　＿＿＿＿＿　　b. 特色
3. scan　　　　　＿＿＿＿＿　　c. 交通工具
4. requirement　　＿＿＿＿＿　　d. 神话
5. scenic spot　　＿＿＿＿＿　　e. 要求
6. specialty　　　＿＿＿＿＿　　f. 招聘
7. renowned　　　＿＿＿＿＿　　g. 景点
8. mystery　　　　＿＿＿＿＿　　h. 报名

9. sign up　　　　　_____　　i. 闻名的

10. masterpiece　　_____　　j. 扫描

II. Fill in the blanks according to the text.

1. _____ will be given at the end of volunteering service.

2. The volunteers will be provided _____.

3. _____ may be allocated to provide services at popular scenic spots.

4. The West Lake is situated in _____.

5. The poet Su Shi in Song Dynasty compared the West Lake to _____.

III. Translate the following sentences according to the dialogue.

1. Volunteers will need to provide assistance, information on cultural, historical, and contemporary heritage, and translations to tourists.

2. All we want is your passion to work at the West Lake, and to learn about the Chinese culture.

3. Volunteers may be allocated to provide services at popular scenic spots such as the Broken Bridge.

4. We provide necessary pre-job training, lunches, and certain transportation subsidies.

5. We are recruiting international volunteers to work at the West Lake.

IV. Work in pairs and discuss the following questions.

1. What impressed you the most in Hangzhou?

2. What do you think about the benefit that the volunteering program provides?

Knowledge Expansion

Hangzhou, China is a tourism hotspot with scenic lakes, thousand-year-old temples, and now a brand new e-sports town complex spanning 3.94 million square feet. That's the size of about 68 football fields.

The e-sports town, operated by the local government, opened its doors to the public on Nov. 16. It cost 2 billion yuan to build, Fox Sports Asia reports. LGD Gaming, a Chinese e-sports organization that owns several successful teams, and Allied Gaming, which owns a network of e-sports arenas around the world, have a joint office and e-sports venue in the complex.

According to an article on People.cn, the city expects the complex to attract more than 10,000 aspiring e-sports professionals and 1 billion yuan in tax revenues. Hangzhou said it plans to build 14 e-sports facilities before 2022 and will invest up to 15.45 billion yuan to do so. These new projects will include a theme park, an e-sports academy, an e-sports-themed hotel, and even a hospital specializing in treating players.

The complex is the first of its kind to open in China. It will not be the last. Chinese company Tencent, the largest video-game company in the world, is building one in the city of Wuhu in east China. It will include an e-sports university and an e-sports theme park, among other facilities. Earlier this year, Taicang, also in east China, announced plans to open an e-sports town.

Hangzhou has an edge on the global stage. The city will play host to the next Asian Games in 2022, where e-sports are expected to be an official medal event (in 2018, it was a demonstration sport). A *Forbes* report estimates that e-sports industry revenues could be \$1.65 billion by 2021 worldwide, and China alone is estimated to drive 18% of total e-sports revenues in 2018. With its investments, Hangzhou is getting ahead in the game.

Invictus Gaming, the Chinese team, thrashed its European rival Fnatic 3-0, taking home the giant silver "Summoner's Cup" and more than \$840,000 in prize money.

E-sports will generate \$906 million in revenue globally this year, according to consultancy Newzoo, while a Goldman Sachs projection suggests 35 percent annual growth and a revenue figure of \$2.96 billion in 2022.

The main winners from e-sports have been game developers, for whom China is their biggest market, according to the consultancy Niko Partners.

"Our optimism and support for e-sports is long term," Tencent's chief operating officer Ren Yuxin told a conference in June. "In the future, we will invest far more resources, personnel and capital in e-sports compared to those in the past."

China is home to more than a dozen professional e-sports teams. But those revenues are outweighed by the rising costs of wages in an increasingly competitive environment. Top players can demand more than 1 million yuan a year in wages, while transfer fees for top players are typically around 1 million yuan — 2 million yuan.

"We are making a loss, but it is less and less each year," said Lu Wenjun, chief executive of Team OMG. "We expect to break even in a year."

Teams are becoming more professionally run. "Wealthy founders realize that it is no longer enough to rely on their own money," said David Ng, EDG's chief executive. "They must introduce investors and find a business model."

参考译文

课文阅读

西湖位于杭州市中心的西部，是江南三大名湖之一。由于西湖的缘故，杭州自古就被誉为"人间天堂"。西湖就像镶嵌在广袤大地上的一颗璀璨的明珠，以其秀丽的风景、著名的古迹、灿烂的文化和丰富的特产而闻名。宋代大文豪苏轼在西湖留下了"欲把西湖比西子，淡妆浓抹总相宜"的千古绝唱；白娘子的传奇故事也给西湖增添了一层神秘色彩。

扩展阅读

中国杭州是一个热门旅游城市，拥有风景如画的湖泊和千年古刹，而现在又有了一个新的电竞数娱小镇。这座小镇占地面积394万平方英尺，大约相当于68个足球场。

电竞数娱小镇由当地政府管理，11月16日向公众开放。据美国福克斯体育亚洲卫视报道称，这个小镇耗资20亿元修建。拥有多支成功团队的中国LGD电子竞技俱乐部以及在全球拥有电子竞技场馆网络的联盟电竞在这个电竞数娱小镇中设有联合办事处以及电竞馆。

据人民网报道，杭州希望电竞数娱小镇将吸引超过1万名有抱负的电子竞技职业选手并带来10亿元人民币的税收。杭州称，电竞数娱小镇计划在2022年前打造14个电竞项目，并将为此投资高达154.5亿元。这些新项目将包括一个主题公园、一所电子竞技学院、一家以电子竞技为主题的酒店，甚至还有一家专门为选手提供治疗的运动康复中心。

这是中国开放的首个电竞数娱小镇，但不会是最后一个。全球最大的视频游戏公司腾讯正在中国东部的芜湖打造电子竞技小镇。该项目将建设一所电子竞技大学和一个电子竞技主题公园等。今年早些时候，同样位于中国东部的太仓市公布了电子竞技小镇建设规划。

杭州在全球舞台上拥有优势。杭州将在2022年主办下一届亚运会，电子竞技预计将成为正式的比赛项目（在2018年亚运会上，电子竞技是表演项目）。据《福布斯》的报道估计，到2021年，全球电子竞技产业的收入可能达到16.5亿美元，而据估计，2018年电子竞技产业总收入的18%就由中国贡献。凭借自身的投资，杭州正在这场比赛中处于领先地位。

在总决赛中，中国的IG战队以3比0战胜欧洲的Fnatic战队，捧回银色的"召唤师杯"以及超过84万美元的奖金。

Newzoo咨询公司的数据显示，电竞今年将在全球带来9.06亿美元收入，高盛公司预测，全球电竞收入将以每年35%的速度增长，并在2022年达到29.6亿美元。

尼科咨询公司称，电竞的最大赢家是游戏开发商，而中国是其最大的市场。

腾讯首席运营官任宇昕在6月的一次会议上说："我们对电竞的乐观态度和支持将是长期的，未来，我们将在电竞领域投入比过去更多的资源、人力和资本。"

中国有十多支职业电竞队,在日益激烈的竞争环境中,工资成本的上涨超过了营收,顶级选手的年薪可能超过 100 万元,而顶级选手的转会费一般在 100 万至 200 万元。

OMG 电子竞技俱乐部总裁陆文俊说:"我们在亏损,但是亏损额每年都在减少,我们希望在一年内实现收支平衡。"

电竞队伍正变得越来越专业化,EDG 电竞俱乐部总裁吴历华说:"有钱的创始人意识到,仅仅依靠自己的钱是不够的。他们必须引入投资者,并找到商业模式。"

参考答案

Exercises

I. 1—5 f c j e g   6—10 b i d h a

II. 1. A volunteer service hours certificate

2. pre-job training, lunches, and certain transportation subsidies

3. Volunteers

4. Hangzhou

5. Xi Shi

III. 1. 志愿者主要是为游客提供帮助,讲述一些文化、历史和当代遗产的信息并翻译。

2. 我们想要的只是你对在西湖工作的热爱,以及对中国文化的了解。

3. 志愿者可能会被分配去"断桥"这些热门景点。

4. 我们会提供必要的入职培训、午餐和一些交通补贴。

5. 我们正在招募国际志愿者到西湖工作。

IV. Omitted

Lesson 2　Jiuzhaigou　九寨沟

Warm-Up

Work in pairs. Learn the following words and phrases. Then answer the following questions.

1. Where is Jiuzhaigou?
2. What is Jiuzhaigou famous for?

➡ Words and Expressions

Read the following words and expressions. Then try to memorize them.

crystal clear 晶莹剔透的，清澈透明的	Tibetan *n.* 西藏人；*a.* 西藏的；西藏人的；西藏文化的
Tibetan food 藏族食品	Tibetan tea 西藏酥油茶
scenic areas 风景名胜区	souvenir *n.* 纪念品

➡ Useful Expressions

1. It's the best place I've ever been to!
2. I wish I could go there. What impressed you the most?
3. Water is the soul of Jiuzhaigou.
4. The water in each lake is very distinctive and crystal clear.
5. What an intoxicating view!
6. I never buy souvenirs in scenic areas because they are too expensive.

➡ Dialogue

Watch the animation, then practice the dialogue by reading it aloud with your partner. Read it through at least twice, and change your role each time.

(**Scene:** Sally is a college student in Cultural and Tourism School from China. Sam is an exchange student from America. Sally just came back from Jiuzhaigou. Sam is very curious about the place.)

Sam: Hi, Sally! I heard that you went to Jiuzhaigou in Sichuan last week?

Sally: Yes, it's the best place I've ever been to!

Sam: Why do you think it's the best?

Sally: Because every sight there is like a painting. Nature really is the best artist.

Sam: I wish I could go there. What impressed you the most?

Sally: I think the water of the colorful lakes.

Sam: Colorful lakes?

Sally: Well, water is the soul of Jiuzhaigou. The water in each lake is very distinctive and crystal clear. Ah, the lakes and the mountains, what an intoxicating view!

Sam: It is said that Sichuan is the hometown of the panda. Did you happen to see one?

Sally: No, but I met some Tibetans, and saw the Tibetans dancing while wearing their traditional clothing. I also ate traditional Tibetan food and drank Tibetan tea.

Sam: Did you buy a souvenir?

Sally: I never buy souvenirs in scenic areas because they are too expensive. But I did buy some Jiuzhaigou beef jerky at a supermarket. It's so delicious! I can share it with you.

Sam: Wow, thank you!

Questions:

1. Where is the hometown of the panda?
2. What is the soul of Jiuzhaigou? Why?

Role-Play

Act it out according to the instructions.

A student from China: Sally

1. To greet Sam and extend welcome to him.
2. Sally tells him what the soul of Jiuzhaigou is, and explains the reason.
3. Sally gives some examples about the animals living in Jiuzhaigou.

A student from America: Sam

1. To greet Sally.
2. To show curiosity about Jiuzhaigou.
3. To ask what the soul of Jiuzhaigou is? And why?

Lesson 2 Jiuzhaigou 九寨沟

🔷 Passage Reading

Jiuzhaigou Nature Reserve, a World Natural Heritage site, is located in the north of Sichuan Province in China. It is the first nature reserve in China with the main purpose of protecting natural scenery. Jiuzhaigou is a valley with a total area of 720 square kilometers. The valley derives its name from the fact that there are 9 ancient Tibetan villages within it. Primeval forests cover more than half of it. There are more than 2,000 kinds of plants in the forest, with a variety of wild animals living there, including 17 national protected species. The first-class protected animals include giant pandas and golden monkeys, and so on. The second-class protected animals include the white-lipped deer, the big swan, etc.

There are 108 beautiful lakes in Jiuzhaigou, and it is said that water is the soul of Jiuzhaigou. The average visibility of the water in the lakes is 12 meters deep, fallen trees and other lake bed sediments are clearly visible and are preserved by the travertine deposits. The crystal clear water is like a necklace decorated in the forests, and the imposing waterfalls are fascinating.

Jiuzhaigou is a great place to visit at any time of the year, and its beauty is beyond the descrption of words. The colorful lakes, the breathtaking trees and mountains, the variations of flora, the cultural landscape of Tibetan wooden buildings… All of these make up a "beautiful fairy tale world".

Useful Words and Expressions:

Jiuzhaigou Nature Reserve 九寨沟自然保护区	World Natural Heritage 世界自然遗产
natural scenery 自然风光	Tibetan villages 藏族山寨
primeval forests 原始森林	national protected species 国家保护物种
panda *n.* 熊猫	golden monkey 金丝猴
visibility *n.* 能见度	lake bed sediments 湖底沉积物
beautiful fairy tale world 美丽的童话世界	

Translation Tasks:

1. 九寨沟自然保护区是世界自然遗产地，位于中国四川省北部。
2. 九寨沟是中国第一个以保护自然风光为主要目的的自然保护区。
3. 九寨沟是一个总面积 720 平方公里的山谷。
4. 原始森林占其中的一半以上。

5. There are more than 2,000 kinds of plants in the forest, with a variety of wild animals living there, including 17 national protected species.

6. The first-class protected animals include pandas and golden monkeys, and so on.

7. It is said that water is the soul of Jiuzhaigou.

8. The average visibility of the water in the lakes is 12 meters deep, fallen trees and other lake bed sediments are clearly visible.

➡ Exercises

I. Match the following words and phrases, and write the corresponding letter for each item.

1. Jiuzhaigou Nature Reserve　_____　　a. 童话世界
2. World Natural Heritage　_____　　b. 金丝猴
3. natural scenery　_____　　c. 熊猫
4. Tibetan villages　_____　　d. 保护物种
5. primeval forests　_____　　e. 九寨沟自然保护区
6. protected species　_____　　f. 能见度
7. panda　_____　　g. 世界自然遗产
8. golden monkey　_____　　h. 自然风光
9. visibility　_____　　i. 藏族山寨
10 fairy tale world　_____　　j. 原始森林

II. Fill in the blanks according to the text.

1. Jiuzhaigou Nature Reserve, a World Natural Heritage site, is located in the north of _____ Province in China.

2. The valley derives its name from the fact that there are 9 ancient _____ villages within it.

3. There are _____ beautiful lakes in Jiuzhaigou, it is said that water is the soul of Jiuzhaigou.

4. There are more than _____ kinds of plants in the forest, with a variety of wild animals living there, including 17 national protected species.

5. It is said that _____ is the hometown of pandas.

III. Translate the following sentences according to the dialogue.

1. Because every sight there is like a painting. Nature really is the best artist.

2. The water in each lake is very distinctive and crystal clear.

3. I met some Tibetans, and saw the Tibetans dancing while wearing their traditional clothing.

4. Did you buy a souvenir?

5. But I did buy some Jiuzhaigou beef jerky at a supermarket.

Ⅳ. *Work in pairs and discuss the following questions.*

1. How do you think of Jiuzhaigou?

2. How do you understand that nature is the best artist?

Knowledge Expansion

Jiuzhaigou is a picturesque fairyland, featuring charming natural scenery of colorful lakes, spectacular waterfalls, and mountains. Located in the mountainous region of southwest China, Jiuzhaigou is not as built-up and busy as the tourist cities of Beijing and Shanghai. Its quiet environment and fresh air attract visitors who are eager to enjoy a beautiful and natural scenic area.

Jiuzhai Valley National Park — a Fairyland

The Jiuzhai Valley National Park is an extravaganza of natural wonders, a pure unspoiled land with waterfalls, alpine lakes, tranquil grasslands, snowy mountain views and Tibetan villages. You'll not believe the fairyland beauty of the area until you've been there and seen it by yourself.

Snowcapped Peaks

Jiuzhaigou has always been famous for its water but the other side of it is the snowcapped peaks that silently guard this fairyland. Every winter, Jiuzhaigou becomes quiet and filled with a poetic and artistic atmosphere. The whole valley and all of the mountains are covered with snow. The ice of the waterfalls and lakes is pure and clean, and the thin streams of water produce a refreshing "music".

Blue Ice

When winter arrives, the flowing waterfalls over the steep rock faces seem to have been affected by the magic of nature, solidifying into a series of stunning ice sheets, ice balls, or icicles. Due to the way the light scatters, the ice — which should be as white as jade — becomes transparently blue. The various forms of blue frozen waterfalls, snowcapped peaks, and clear blue lakes comprise a beautiful and magical snow world. It is said that the blue ice phenomenon is very rare. It appears only at the end of January and early February every year for about a dozen days.

(Excerpted from www. bing. com)

参考译文

课文阅读

九寨沟自然保护区是世界自然遗产地,位于中国四川省北部。它是中国第一个以保护自然风光为主要目的的自然保护区。九寨沟是一个总面积 720 平方公里的山谷。山谷的名字源于山谷内部有 9 个古老的藏族山寨。原始森林占其中的一半以上。森林中有 2,000 多种植物,这里生活着各种野生动物,包括 17 种国家保护物种。一级保护动物包括大熊猫和金丝猴等。二级保护动物包括白唇鹿和大天鹅等。

九寨沟有 108 个美丽的湖泊,据说水是九寨沟的灵魂。湖泊中水的平均能见度为 12 米,倒下的树木和其他湖床沉积物清晰可见。清澈的水就像是在森林里装饰的项链,瀑布很迷人。

九寨沟是一年中任何时候都可以参观的好地方,九寨沟的美丽无法言喻。五彩缤纷的湖泊、令人叹为观止的树木和山脉、植被的变化、藏族木制建筑的文化景观……所有这些构成了一个"美丽的童话世界"。

扩展阅读

九寨沟是一个风景如画的仙境,拥有五彩缤纷的湖泊、壮观的瀑布和群山的迷人自然风光。九寨沟位于中国西南山区,不如北京和上海的旅游城市那么繁忙。安静的环境和新鲜的空气吸引了渴望享受美丽自然风景区的游客。

九寨沟国家公园——仙境

九寨沟国家公园是自然奇观的盛会,是一片纯净的未受污染的土地,有瀑布、高山湖泊、宁静的草原、雪山景色和藏族村庄。除非你亲自去过那里,否则你不会相信该地区的仙境之美。

白雪皑皑的山峰

九寨沟一直以其水而闻名,但另一端是白雪皑皑的山峰,默默守护着这个仙境。每年冬天,九寨沟都会变得安静,充满诗意和艺术氛围,整个山谷和所有山脉都被白雪覆盖。瀑布和湖泊的冰块纯洁干净,稀薄的水流产生令人耳目一新的"音乐"。

蓝冰

到了冬天,陡峭的岩石表面上流淌的瀑布似乎受到了自然"魔力"的影响,固化成一系列令人惊叹的冰盖、冰球或冰柱。由于光线的散射，应该像玉一样白的冰变成透明的蓝色。各种形式的蓝色冰冻瀑布、白雪皑皑的山峰和湛蓝的湖泊构成了美丽而神奇的雪世界。据说蓝冰现象非常罕见。它仅在每年的 1 月底和 2 月初出现，大约持续 12 天。

参考答案

Exercises

Ⅰ. 1—5　e g h i j　　6—10　d c b f a

Ⅱ. 1. Sichuan

2. Tibetan

3. 108

4. 2,000

5. Sichuan

Ⅲ. 1. 因为那里的每一个景色都像一幅画。大自然确实是最好的艺术家。

2. 每个湖中的水都非常独特且清澈。

3. 我遇到了一些藏族人，看到他们穿着传统服装跳舞。

4. 您买了纪念品吗？

5. 但是我确实在一家超市买了一些九寨沟牛肉干。

Ⅳ. Omitted

Unit IV
Historical Sites
历史古迹

Lesson 1　The Great Wall　长城

Warm-Up

Work in pairs. Learn the following words and phrases. Then answer the following questions.

1. Have you ever been to the Great Wall? How was your experience?
2. How long is the Great Wall of China?
3. Why was it built?

➡ Words and Expressions

Read the following words and expressions. Then try to memorize them.

border *n.* 国界，边界	invader *n.* 入侵者
stretch *v.* 拉长，伸展	military *a.* 军事的，军队的
parallel *a.* 平行的，对应的	steep *a.* 陡峭的
a must-see 必看的东西，不容错过的景点	exhausted *a.* 筋疲力尽的
range from 范围从……到……	

➡ Useful Expressions

1. The original wall was ordered by the Emperor Qin to be built over 2000 years ago.
2. The Great Wall is actually a system of walls, some built parallel to each other for greater strength and security.
3. The Great Wall is the longest man-made structure ever built.
4. The main purpose of the Great Wall was to protect China from invasion or attack by northern tribes.
5. One who fails to reach the Great Wall is not a hero.
6. You can visit the Great Wall of China throughout the year but visiting it in summer is not recommended.

Lesson 1　The Great Wall　长城

➡ Dialogue

Watch the animation, then practice the dialogue by reading it aloud with your partner. Read it through at least twice, and change your role each time.

(**Scene:** Sally is a college student in Cultural and Tourism School from China. Sam is an exchange student from America. Sam is seeking advice from Sally about visiting the Great Wall of China.)

Sam: Sally, I need your advice.
Sally: Of course.
Sam: Well, a friend of mine is visiting Beijing. He wants to see the Great Wall.
Sally: The best time to visit the Great Wall around Beijing is spring or autumn.
Sam: You mean to avoid the hot and crowded summer, and the freezing conditions of winter?
Sally: Correct.
Sam: Any suggestions on how to get there?
Sally: You have to decide if you want to travel solo or in a group.
Sam: Well, I like to set off on my own. Do you know how I can get there?
Sally: I know there's a small station outside the west gate of Beijing University of Aeronautics and Astronautics, but I've never been there before. You may go there and ask around.
Sam: That's very close to where I live. I'll check it out! By the way, have you ever been to the Great Wall?
Sally: Yes, I have. It is very impressive! Visiting the Great Wall is almost like climbing a mountain! Looking out from the Great Wall, you can really get a sense of history.
Sam: Great! I'm really looking forward to it. So, Sally, since you've been to the Great Wall, you are a "true man", right?
Sally: Yes, now I drink lots of beer and even smoke cigars!
Sam: Really?
Sally: Of course not, I'm just kidding!

Questions:
1. What is the best time to visit the Great Wall?
2. Is it physically tough to climb the Great Wall?
3. Do you think going solo to the Great Wall is a good idea?
4. How can Sam get to the Great Wall?

Role-Play

Act it out according to the instructions.

A student in China: Sally

1. Greets Sam in a casual way.
2. Gives Sam some advice on visiting the Great Wall.
3. Answers questions from Sam.

A student from America: Sam

1. Greets Sally in a casual way.
2. Seeks advice on visiting the Great Wall.
3. Asks how to get to the Great Wall.

Passage Reading

- How long is the Great Wall of China?

The Great Wall of China is approximately 21,169.18 kilometres long. However if you were to measure all the individual structures and changes to the wall made over the centuries, it is believed the final measurement would total over 50,000 kilometres!

- When was the Great Wall of China built?

The Great Wall was originally built over 2,000 years ago, around 221 BC. Most of the current Great Wall was built during the Ming Dynasty (between 1368 and 1644).

- Why was the Great Wall of China built?

It is believed that the main purpose of the Great Wall was to protect China from invasion or attack by northern tribes.

- How long did it take to build the Great Wall of China?

The Great Wall was built over many years. It is believed the original Great Wall was built over a period of approximately 20 years. The Great Wall which is mainly in evidence today was actually built during the Ming Dynasty, over a period of around 200 years.

- How many people did it take to build the Great Wall of China?

Many thousands of people were involved in the building of the wall. From records it appears that 300,000 soldiers and 500,000 common people were involved in constructing the original Great Wall under Emperor Qin. Many people lost their lives during this work.

Lesson 1　The Great Wall　长城

Useful Words and Expressions：

measure *v.* 测量，度量

evidence *n.* 根据，证明

involve *v.* 加入，参与，涉及

attack *v.* 袭击，攻击

construct *v.* 建筑，修建

approximately *ad.* 大概，大约

Translation Tasks:

1. 长城大约 21,196.18 千米长。

2. 长城始建于 2,000 年前。

3. 建造长城的主要目的是保护中国不受侵犯。

4. Most of the current Great Wall was built during the Ming Dynasty.

5. It is believed the original Great Wall was built over a period of approximately 20 years.

6. Many thousands of people were involved in the building of the wall.

7. Many people lost their lives during this work.

Exercises

Ⅰ. *Match the following words and phrases, and write the corresponding letter for each item.*

1. attack　　＿＿＿＿＿＿　　a. 袭击
2. protect　　＿＿＿＿＿＿　　b. 建造
3. involve　　＿＿＿＿＿＿　　c. 参加
4. record　　＿＿＿＿＿＿　　d. 保护
5. measure　＿＿＿＿＿＿　　e. 测量
6. construct　＿＿＿＿＿＿　　f. 记录

Ⅱ. *Fill in the blanks according to the text.*

1. Most of the Great Wall we see today was actually built during ＿＿＿＿＿＿.

2. The primary motive of its construction was to protect China from ＿＿＿＿＿＿.

3. It is believed the original Great Wall was built over a period of ＿＿＿＿＿＿.

4. Thousands of people were involved in constructing the original Great Wall ordered by ＿＿＿＿＿＿.

5. The length of the Great Wall is ＿＿＿＿＿＿.

Ⅲ. *Translate the following sentences according to the dialogue.*

1. The best time to visit the Great Wall around Beijing is spring or autumn.

2. You mean to avoid the hot and crowded summer, and the freezing conditions of winter?

3. You have to decide if you want to travel solo or in a group.

4. I like to set off on my own.

5. 你去过长城吗？

6. 那里离我住的地方很近。

7. 游览长城就像爬山一样。

8. 我真的很期待游览长城。

Ⅳ. *Work in pairs and discuss the following questions.*

1. Should you travel solo or in a group?

2. Can you walk all over the Great Wall?

Knowledge Expansion

Is the Great Wall truly visible from the moon? Yang Liwei, China's first astronaut who was lifted into the outer space by the spacecraft Shenzhou V on Oct. 15, 2003, gave a definite answer "No" to a reporter after he reached the ground. Yang's negative response in a practical way may probably put out a fair number of people's passion. But it powerfully corrected the misconception. The Great Wall is indeed majestic, but you won't see it from the space!

In fact, besides Yang Liwei, there are a lot of astronauts said the Great Wall could not be seen from the space. Neil Alden Armstrong, the American aviator who first set foot on the moon in 1969, was asked a thousand times whether or not he had seen the Great Wall from the moon. In a sound recording from NASA Johnson Space Center, Armstrong said that he had seen the continents, lakes and blue spots touched with red. But he could not make out any man-made object on the earth from the moon.

What's more, Buzz Aldrin, one of the two American astronauts besides Neil Alden Armstrong that first landed on the moon, insisted that the wrong statement was from people's misunderstanding. Jeffrey Alan Hoffman claimed that he had not seen the Wall though much time was spent to overlook the earth, including many moments skimming over China's airspace. Dennis Anthony Tito, the first space tourist from America who spent the space vacation in 2001, also said the Great Wall is invisible from the space.

Theoretically speaking, the Great Wall is absolutely invisible from the space. It is narrow and irregular. In space, something irregular is hard to be observed. Measuring about 10 meters wide on average, it is easily immerged into the surrounding environment. Depending solely on

Lesson 1　The Great Wall　长城

unaided eyes, it is hardly distinguished at an altitude of 65,617 feet. It is totally invisible at a height of 196,850 feet. To watch the wall on the moon is equivalent to seeking for a single hair from 2,688 meters away. To say an astronaut can see the Great Wall from the space is obviously not true.

参考译文

课文阅读

- 长城有多长？

长城长约 21196.18 千米。但是，如果把过去几个世纪的工程和改造都纳入测量的话，相信最终的测量将超过 50,000 千米！

- 长城是什么时候建造的？

长城最初建于 2,000 多年前，大约公元前 221 年。现在的长城大部分建于明朝（1368 年至 1644 年）。

- 为什么要建造长城？

人们认为长城的主要目的是保护中国免受北方部落的入侵或攻击。

- 建造长城花了多少时间？

长城是用很多年建成的。据说，原来的长城是在大约 20 年的时间内建成的。今天现存的长城实际上建于明朝，历时约 200 年。

- 多少人参与了长城的建造？

成千上万的人参与了这堵墙的修建。据记载，秦始皇时期有 30 万士兵、50 万平民参与修建长城。许多人在这项工程中丧生。

扩展阅读

从月球上真的能看见长城吗？2003 年 10 月 15 日，中国第一位乘坐神舟五号载人飞船的航天员杨利伟在到达地面后，干脆利落地回答："不能。"他的回应浇灭了相当一部分人的热情。但这句回应有力地纠正了人们的误解。长城确实很雄伟，但从太空是看不到它的！

其实，除了杨利伟，还有很多航天员说从太空看不到长城。1969 年首次踏上月球的美国飞行员尼尔·奥尔登·阿姆斯特朗曾被无数次问及是否从月球上看到过长城。美国宇航局约翰逊航天中心公布的一段录音中，阿姆斯特朗说，他看到了大陆、湖泊和蓝色斑点被染成了红色。但他无法从月球上辨认出地球上的任何人造物体。

另外，除了尼尔·奥尔登·阿姆斯特朗之外，其他两位登陆月球的美国宇航员也表述了他们的所见。巴兹·奥尔德林坚称，错误的说法来自人们的误解。杰弗里·阿兰·霍夫曼声称虽然他花了很多时间俯瞰地球，包括许多掠过中国领空的瞬间，但他没有看到长城。丹尼斯·安东尼·蒂托是第一位在 2001 年进行太空度假的美国太空游客，他也说，太空中看不见长城。

从理论上讲，长城从太空中看是绝对看不见的，它既窄又不规则。在太空中，不规则的东西很难被观察到。长城平均宽约 10 米，很容易隐没在周围环境中，很难在 65,617 英尺（约 20,000 米）的高空仅靠肉眼分辨。它在 196,850 英尺（约 60,000 米）的高度是完全看不见的。从月球上看长城相当于从 2,688 米外寻找一根头发。因此，宇航员能够从太空中看到长城的说法是不正确的。

参考答案

Exercises

Ⅰ. 1—6　a d c f e b

Ⅱ. 1. the Ming Dynasty

　　2. invasion or attack

　　3. approximately 20 years

　　4. Emperor Qin

　　5. 21,196.18 kilometres long

Ⅲ. 1. 在北京游览长城的最佳时间是春秋两季。

　　2. 你的意思是避开炎热拥挤的夏天和拥挤的人群，以及寒冷的冬天？

　　3. 你必须决定是独自旅行还是集体旅行。

　　4. 我喜欢自行出发。

　　5. Have you ever been to the Great Wall?

　　6. That's very close to where I live.

　　7. Visiting the Great Wall is almost like climbing a mountain!

　　8. I'm really looking forward to visiting the Great Wall.

Ⅳ. Omitted

Lesson 2　The Forbidden City　紫禁城

Warm-Up

Work in pairs. Learn the following words and phrases. Then answer the following questions.

1. Have you watched a program relating to the Forbidden City by Beijing TV station?
2. What impressed you the most in the Forbidden City?

Words and Expressions

Read the following words and expressions. Then try to memorize them.

complex *n*. 复合体；综合设施　　scenic *a*. 风景优美的
spot *n*. 地点；斑点　　highlight *n*. 最精彩的部分；强调

Useful Expressions

1. I want to know more about Beijing's scenic spots.
2. Is it a must-see highlight for every first-time visitor to Beijing?
3. A piece of advice I could give you is to be prepared for crowds of people.
4. There are two entrances to the Forbidden City.

Dialogue

Watch the animation, then practice the dialogue by reading it aloud with your partner. Read it through at least twice, and change your role each time.

(**Scene:** Sally is a college student in Cultural and Tourism School from China. Sam is an exchange student from America. Sam wants to know something more about scenic spots in Beijing.)

Sam: Hi, Sally! I want to know more about Beijing's scenic spots.
Sally: Have you ever been to the Forbidden City? Well, personally I love this particular scenic spot very much.

Sam: Is it a must-see highlight for every first-time visitor to Beijing?

Sally: Definitely. A piece of advice I could give you is to be prepared for crowds of people, and try to avoid visiting there on weekends or public holidays.

Sam: That's terrible!

Sally: Yes, but it's true.

Sam: What's the opening time?

Sally: Well, it opens daily. Different seasons do have different times, so you'd better go early in the morning to avoid the crowds.

Sam: Got it.

Sally: Well, there are two entrances to the Forbidden City: The northern gate and the southern gate. The northern gate is less crowded.

Sam: How long does it take to walk through the entire palace?

Sally: It takes two or three hours, because the Forbidden City is a huge complex, covering 72 hectares.

Sam: Thank you for your suggestions!

Sally: My pleasure. Have a great time.

Sam: Bye!

Questions:

1. How many entrances does the Forbidden City have?
2. Does the Forbidden City have a fixed opening hour?

Role-Play

Act it out according to the instructions.

A student from China: Sally

1. Greetings.
2. Sally suggests that he go to the Forbidden City.
3. Sally tells him the Forbidden City is very popular, so choosing a proper time to visit is necessary in order to avoid the crowds.

A student from America: Sam

1. Greetings.
2. Sam wants to visit some places of interest in Beijing.
3. Sam gets some suggestions from Sally.

Lesson 2　The Forbidden City　紫禁城

🔹 Passage Reading

The Palace Museum, known as the Forbidden City, was the imperial palaces of the Ming and Qing Dynasties. The construction took 14 years and was completed in 1420. In the following year, the capital of the Ming Dynasty was moved from Nanjing to Beijing. There are 24 emperors of the Ming and Qing Dynasties ruling from the Forbidden City. The palace is the largest piece of the ancient Chinese architecture existing at present. The palace had been expanded several times, but the original layout was preserved. After 1949, some renovations were done and the Palace Museum was listed as one of the important historical monuments under special preservation by the Chinese government.

Useful Words and Expressions:

imperial *a.* 皇帝的；帝国的	architecture *n.* 建筑；建筑风格
layout *n.* 布局	expand *v.* 扩张
renovation *n.* 翻修	the Palace Museum 故宫

Translation Tasks:

1. 故宫曾经是明代和清代的皇家宫殿。
2. 明代和清代 24 位皇帝曾经住在紫禁城内，进行统治。
3. 这座宫殿是仍然屹立的最大的中国古代建筑。
4. The palace had been expanded several times, but the original layout was preserved.

🔹 Exercises

Ⅰ. *Match the following words and phrases, and write the corresponding letter for each item.*

1. imperial　　_____　　a. 故宫
2. entire　　　_____　　b. 建筑群
3. complex　　_____　　c. 帝王的
4. highlight　 _____　　d. 布局
5. layout　　　_____　　e. 君主
6. the Palace Museum _____ f. 保护
7. emperor　　_____　　g. 整个的
8. renovation　_____　　h. 建设

9. preservation　　　　＿＿＿＿＿＿　　　i. 强调

10. construction　　　　＿＿＿＿＿＿　　　j. 翻修

II. Fill in the blanks according to the text.

1. The Forbidden City has two entrances, ＿＿＿＿＿＿＿＿＿＿＿＿.
2. If you walk through the whole palace, you will take ＿＿＿＿＿＿.
3. The Forbidden City is also known as ＿＿＿＿＿＿.
4. The Palace Museum is ＿＿＿＿＿ Chinese ancient complex existing now.
5. In 1421, the capital of Ming Dynasty was moved to ＿＿＿＿＿.

III. Translate the following sentences according to the dialogue.

1. Different seasons do have different times, so you'd better go early in the morning to avoid the crowds.
2. Is it a must-see highlight for every first-time visitor to Beijing?
3. It takes two or three hours, because the Forbidden City is a huge complex, covering 72 hectares.
4. A piece of advice I could give you is to be prepared for crowds of people, and try to avoid visiting there on weekends or public holidays.

IV. Work in pairs and discuss the following questions.

1. If you were living in the Qing Dynasty, can you adapt to the lifestyle?
2. Can you briefly introduce a national treasure you are interested in of the Forbidden City?

▶ Knowledge Expansion

A special exhibition will be held by the Palace Museum to celebrate the upcoming Chinese New Year, Xinhua reports.

Starting January 6, 2019, the first of the twelfth lunar month in Chinese calendar, a record-breaking number of around 1,000 antique items will reportedly be displayed at the famed museum.

The former record is currently held by the 1935 International Exhibition of Chinese Art in London, where 735 antiques from the museum were showcased.

The exhibition will be divided into six areas, fully displaying the customs of the Chinese New Year during the Qing Dynasty, with an open area decorated with historical customs of the dynasty and restored "royal" festival celebration activities.

"The exhibition will not only present the visitors with antique collections, but will also allow the audience to immerse themselves in the cultural atmosphere of ancient China," said Shan Jixiang, former curator of the museum.

During the exhibition, the museum will be embellished with traditional Chinese New Year decorations such as Spring Festival couplets and lanterns.

参考译文

课文阅读

故宫,也称紫禁城,曾经是明代和清代的皇家宫殿。故宫的建设历经14年,于1420年完工。次年,明代的都城从南京迁到了北京。明代和清代24位皇帝曾经在紫禁城进行统治。这座宫殿仍然是屹立的最大的中国古代建筑。故宫曾经历了几次扩建,但原有布局始终得以保留。1949年之后,故宫进行了一些修缮,同时被中国政府列为重要的历史遗迹之一,得到特殊保护。

扩展阅读

据新华社报道,为庆祝即将到来的春节,故宫博物院将举办一场特别展览。

本次展览将于2019年1月6日开幕,正值农历腊月初一,破纪录的近千件文物将在这个著名的博物馆展出。

之前的纪录是由1935年在伦敦举行的"中国艺术国际展览会"保持的,共展出了735件文物。

本次展览将分为六大主题,全面展现清代宫廷的过年习俗。在一个开放的区域里装饰着清代的历史习俗,重现"皇家"节日庆祝活动。

时任故宫博物院院长单霁翔表示:"这次展览不仅将向参观者展示文物收藏品,而且还将使观众沉浸在中国古代的文化氛围中。"

在展览期间,故宫博物院将用中国传统的新年装饰品,如春联和灯笼来进行装饰。

参考答案

Exercises

I. 1—5 c g b i d   6—10 a e j f h

II. 1. the northern gate and the southern gate

2. two or three hours

3. the Palace Museum

4. the largest

5. Beijing

Ⅲ. 1. 不同的季节有不同的时间，所以你最好早上去，以避免拥挤。

2. 它是每个第一次来北京的游客必看的景点吗？

3. 那可能需要两三个小时，因为紫禁城是一个占地72公顷的巨大建筑群。

4. 我可以给你的一个建议是，一定要做好面对人潮的心理准备，尽量避免在周末或公共假日去那里。

Ⅳ. Omitted

Unit V
Quintessence
of Chinese Culture
经典国粹

Lesson 1　Calligraphy　书法

Warm-Up

Work in pairs. Learn the following words and phrases. Then answer the following questions.

1. Did you learn calligraphy when you were a child?
2. Do you like hard-tipped pen writing or traditional brush writing?

➡ Words and Expressions

Read the following words and expressions. Then try to memorize them.

regular *a.* 有规律的；定期的	wonderful *a.* 极好的；精彩的
script *n.* 剧本；手迹	treasure *n.* 珍宝；财富

➡ Useful Expressions

1. There's a Calligraphy Contest next month on campus.
2. There are so many scripts, such as seal script, official script, cursives cript, and regular script.
3. They are the basic tools for calligraphy.
4. I have been looking for one too.
5. They're called the "four treasures of the study": writing brush, ink stick, paper, and ink stone.

➡ Dialogue

Watch the animation, then practice the dialogue by reading it aloud with your partner. Read it through at least twice, and change your role each time.

(**Scene:** Sally is a college student in Cultural and Tourism School from China. Sam is an exchange student from America. Sally has become fascinated with calligraphy these days.)

Sam: Sally, what are you doing?

Lesson 1   Calligraphy   书法

Sally: I'm practicing Chinese calligraphy.

Sam: Good writing. It's beautiful.

Sally: Thanks. I bought some books about calligraphy.

Sam: Oh, I have been looking for one too. Where did you get them?

Sally: At the international bookstore. There's a Calligraphy Contest next month on campus. Do you know that?

Sam: Yeah, it's wonderful. What are these things?

Sally: They are the basic tools for calligraphy. They're called the "four treasures of the study": writing brush, ink stick, paper, and ink stone.

Sam: Are you serious?

Sally: Sure. I love it. There are so many scripts, such as seal script, official script, cursive script, and regular script.

Sam: Which one are you working on?

Sally: The regular script.

Sam: That's great! Can you teach me?

Sally: No problem.

Questions:

1. What are the "four treasures of the study"?
2. What script is Sally practicing?

➡ Role-Play

Act it out according to the instructions.

A student from China: Sally

1. Greetings.
2. Sally is preparing to participate in the contest of calligraphy next month.
3. Sally promises to teach him.

A student from America: Sam

1. Greetings.
2. Sam is curious about what the "four treasures of the study" are.
3. Sam wants to learn Chinese calligraphy, too.

🔸 Passage Reading

Chinese calligraphy is not only a traditional method of Chinese character writing with a long history, but also an art of self-cultivation and self-expression. The inner world of the writer could be reflected with the help of the beautiful Chinese script. Chinese calligraphy plays an important role in Chinese art, for it has influenced other Chinese artistic forms like classical poetry, sculpture, traditional music and dance, architecture and handicrafts. As a treasured artistic form of Chinese culture, Chinese calligraphy is enjoyed by people throughout the world and is becoming more and more popular.

Useful Words and Expressions:

self-cultivation 自我修养
self-expression 自我表现
inner world 内心世界
classical poetry 古典诗歌
handicraft n. 手工艺品

Translation Tasks:

1. 中国书法不仅是汉字的传统书写形式，也是体现自我修养和自我表达的艺术。
2. 中国书法被全世界人民所喜爱。
3. The inner world of the writer could be reflected with the help of the beautiful Chinese script.
4. It has influenced other Chinese artistic forms like classical poetry, sculpture, traditional music and dance, architecture and handicrafts.

🔸 Exercises

Ⅰ. *Match the following words and phrases, and write the corresponding letter for each item.*

1. cursive　　　　　_____　　a. 脚本
2. seal　　　　　　_____　　b. 雕塑
3. regular　　　　　_____　　c. 印章
4. script　　　　　 _____　　d. 手工艺
5. contest　　　　　_____　　e. 定期的
6. classical poetry　_____　　f. 艺术的
7. sculpture　　　　_____　　g. 比赛
8. artistic　　　　　_____　　h. 自我修养

9. self-cultivation　　　　_____　　i. 草书的

10. handicraft　　　　　　_____　　j. 古典诗歌

II. Fill in the blanks according to the text.

1. _____ is one of artistic forms of Chinese culture.

2. The beautiful Chinese calligraphy can reflect _____.

3. The basic tools for calligraphy are _____.

4. There are so many scripts, such as _____ and so on.

5. Chinese calligraphy has great effect on other _____.

III. Translate the following sentences according to the dialogue.

1. They're called the "four treasures of the study": writing brush, ink stick, paper, and ink stone.

2. There are so many scripts, such as seal script, official script, cursive script, and regular script.

3. Which one are you working on?

4. There's a calligraphy contest next month on campus.

IV. Work in pairs and discuss the following questions.

1. How do you think practicing calligraphy can promote self-cultivation?

2. Can you describe the evolution of Chinese characters?

➡ Knowledge Expansion

Writing Brush

The earliest writing brush that has been found is a relic of the Warring States Period (475 BC—221 BC). From that time onwards, the brush has evolved into many forms. The nib can be made from rabbit's hair, wool, horsehair, weasel's hair, or bristles, and so on; while the shaft may be made from bamboo, ivory, jade, crystal, gold, silver, porcelain, sandal, ox horn, etc. It is important to see that there can be both soft and hard brushes, each of which produces its own particular style.

The delicacy gives painters inspiration for creation, and has led to brush shafts being decorated with artistic patterns. One prized example was an ivory-weasel's hair writing brush. On the ivory shaft with the diameter of 0.8 cm, there are carved eight figures of the immortals and pavilions seemingly concealed in the clouds. With this in one's hand, the threads of writing would hardly halt.

Ink Stick

A good ink stick should be grouned so as to be refined black with luster. With the invention of paper, they were improved accordingly. Since the Han Dynasty (206 BC—220), ink sticks have been made from pine soot, using other procedures that include mixing with glue, steaming and molding. In ancient times, emperors such as Qianlong in the Qing Dynasty (1644—1911) had paid great attention to the production of ink sticks and were expert in their appreciation of quality inks.

Paper

Paper making is among the "four great inventions" and one of the great contributions that ancient Chinese people made to the world.

It was Cai Lun who made the valuable contribution and his research gave rise to paper. Afterwards, many varieties of paper of different quality and usage were produced. Today the Xuan paper originally made in Anhui Province still shines with its charm.

Ink Slab

The ink slab is the reputed head of the "four treasures", for its sobriety and elegance has endured the passage of time. Through ink slabs, people can sample the artistic charm of sculpting and the ink stone's natural tints. Nearly all Chinese calligraphy enthusiasts hold that the star of ink slab is the Duanyan, the ink slab produced in Duanzhou of Guangdong Province. It has a purple hue on its base and enjoys the poetic name 'purple clouds'. It was always a tribute to the royal families during the Tang Dynasty (618—907).

参考译文

课文阅读

中国书法历史悠久，它不仅是汉字的传统书写形式，也是体现自我修养和自我表达的艺术。作者的内心世界通过美妙的字体得以体现。书法在中国艺术中拥有举足轻重的地位，因为它影响到了其他的中国艺术形式，如古典诗歌、雕塑、传统音乐及舞蹈、建筑及手工艺品。作为传统的艺术瑰宝，中国书法被全世界人民所喜爱，且越来越受到欢迎。

扩展阅读

毛笔

人们发现的最早的毛笔是战国时期（公元前475年—公元前221年）的遗物。从那时起，毛笔就演变成多种形式。笔尖可以用兔毛、羊毛、马毛、黄鼠狼毛或猪鬃等制成；轴可由竹子、象牙、玉石、水晶、金、银、瓷器、檀香、牛角等制成。很重要的一点是，软笔刷和硬笔刷各有其独特的风格。

这种精致给了画家创作的灵感,并由此产生了毛笔轴装饰艺术图案。一个很好的例子就是象牙狼毫毛笔。在直径0.8厘米的象牙塔上,雕刻着八位神仙和亭台楼阁,仿佛隐没在云雾之中。手握此笔,便会才思泉涌。

墨棒

好墨应细磨,使之黑而有光泽。随着纸的发明,它们得到了相应的改进。从汉朝(公元前206年—220年)开始,墨棒就由松烟灰制成,使用的其他方法包括与胶水混合、蒸和成型。在古代,清朝(1636—1911)的乾隆皇帝非常重视墨棒的生产,并擅长鉴赏高质量的墨水。

纸

造纸术是"四大发明"之一,是中国古代人民对世界的伟大贡献之一。正是蔡伦做出了宝贵的贡献,他研究出了纸。后来,许多不同质量和用途的纸张被生产出来。今天,安徽的宣纸依然散发着它的魅力。

砚台

砚台被誉为"文房四宝"之首,因为它的庄严和典雅经受了时间的考验。通过砚台,人们可以领略到雕刻的艺术魅力和水墨的自然色彩。几乎所有的中国书法爱好者都认为,砚台之星是产自广东端州的"端砚"。它的底色是紫色的,因此得名"紫云"。在唐朝(618—907),它一直是皇室的贡品。

参考答案

Exercises

Ⅰ. 1—5 i c e a g   6—10 j b f h d

Ⅱ. 1. Chinese calligraphy

2. writer's inner world

3. writing brush, ink stick, paper, and ink stone

4. seal script, official script, cursive script, regular script

5. other artistic forms of Chinese culture

Ⅲ. 1. 它们被称为"文房四宝":毛笔、墨、纸、砚。

2. 中国有篆书、隶书、草书、楷书等多种书写体。

3. 你在练哪一种字体呢?

4. 下个月校园里有一场书法比赛。

Ⅳ. Omitted

Lesson 2　Peking Opera　京剧

Warm-Up

Work in pairs. Learn the following words and phrases. Then answer the following questions.

1. Can you say something about Peking Opera?
2. Character roles in Peking Opera are generally divided into four main types according to the sex, age, social status and profession of the character. What are they?

Words and Expressions

Read the following words and expressions. Then try to memorize them.

pretentiously *ad.* 装腔作势地，做作地	conqueror *n.* 征服者；占领者；胜利者
corner *n.* 街角；拐角；困境；窘境；	
v. 迫至一隅；使陷入绝境	personality *n.* 个性，品格
facial makeup 脸谱	in despair 绝望地
commit suicide 自杀	

Useful Expressions

1. You have been sitting here watching for a long time.
2. It seems that you are watching something interesting!
3. They are colorfully dressed and painted.
4. In despair, his beloved wife Yuji chooses to commit suicide.
5. The actors and actresses in Peking Opera all wear facial makeup.
6. It symbolizes loyalty and courage.

Dialogue

Watch the animation, then practice the dialogue by reading it aloud with your partner. Read it through at least twice, and change your role each time.

Lesson 2 Peking Opera 京剧

(**Scene:** Sally is a college student in Cultural and Tourism School from China. Sam is an exchange student from America. Sally is watching Peking Opera. Sam is very curious about it.)

Sam: Hi, Sally! You have been sitting here watching for a long time. It seems that you are watching something interesting! What are you watching? A new film?

Sally: No, it's Peking Opera, the story of *Farewell to My Concubine*.

Sam: Peking Opera? Who's that beautiful woman?

Sally: She's Yuji, Xiang Yu's wife.

Sam: Oh, They are colorfully dressed and painted, and they act rather… pretentiously on the stage. What's the story about?

Sally: It's a beautiful love story, about the Conqueror Xiang Yu, a famous general who rebelled against the Qin Dynasty and overthrew it. Later he is cornered by the leader of another group, Liu Bang. In despair, his beloved wife Yuji chooses to commit suicide by stabbing herself with a knife.

Sam: Oh, it's so sad! Look! Xiang Yu is wearing a black and white mask, I can't understand why…

Sally: No, it's not a mask, it's facial makeup. The actors and actresses in Peking Opera all wear facial makeups that indicate their personalities. The black color symbolizes firmness and honesty, a white face symbolizes cruelty, while a black and white face shows a defeated hero who is brave, cocky and foolhardy.

Sam: How about a red one?

Sally: It symbolizes loyalty and courage.

Questions:

1. What is the story *Farewell to My Concubine* about?
2. What color is Xiang Yu's facial makeup? Can you tell the reason?
3. What does a red facial makeup symbolize?
4. Who is Xiang Yu?

➡ Role-Play

Act it out according to the instructions.

A student from China: Sally

1. To greet Sam and extend welcome to him.

2. Sally tells him some knowledge about Peking Opera, and explains the story of *Farewell to My Concubine*.
3. Sally tells him what different facial makeups symbolize.

A student from America: Sam

1. To greet Sally.
2. To show curiosity about Peking Opera.
3. To ask how to tell an actor's personality by his facial makeup.

Passage Reading

Peking Opera is a traditional form of Chinese theatre. It combines music, dance, acrobatics and vocal performance. Character roles in Peking Opera are generally divided into four main types according to the sex, age, social status and profession of the character. They are Sheng, Dan, Jing, Chou. Facial make-up date far back in history. In ancient time, actors wore masks when playing Peking Opera, later, facial make-up replaced the mask. From the facial make-up, we can instantly tell the personalities of the characters.

Li Yuan, the best place to enjoy Peking Opera, literally means pear garden in Chinese and also refer to the place where opera players are trained. Many Peking Opera masters often play here.

Since Mei Lanfang, the grand master of Peking Opera, visited Japan in 1919, Peking Opera has become more and more popular with people all over the world. It has made an excellent contribution to cultural exchange between China and the West. Nowadays, you can catch traveling troupes of Peking Opera performers in many international cities and local "Chinatowns".

Useful Words and Expressions:

Chinese theatre 中国曲艺	male character 男性角色
female character 女性角色	male character with a painted face 花脸
clown n. 喜剧角色	facial make-up 京剧脸谱
personality of character 人物性格	

Translation Tasks:

1. 京剧是中国曲艺的传统形式。
2. 根据角色的性别、年龄、社会地位和职业,京剧中的角色一般分为四种主要类型。
3. 京剧脸谱的历史要追溯到很久以前。

4. 在古代，演员在表演京剧时都戴着面具，后来，脸谱取代了面具。

5. From the facial make-up, we can instantly tell the personalities of the characters.

6. It combines music, dance, acrobatics and vocal performance.

7. They are Sheng, Dan, Jing, Chou, that is, male character, female character, male character with a painted face and clown.

8. Later, facial make-up replaced the mask.

➡ Exercises

Ⅰ. *Match the following words and phrases, and write the corresponding letter for each item.*

1. Chinese theatre　　＿＿＿＿＿　　a. 自杀
2. clown　　＿＿＿＿＿　　b. 绝望地
3. mask　　＿＿＿＿＿　　c. 脸谱
4. personality of character　　＿＿＿＿＿　　d. 男性角色
5. pretentiously　　＿＿＿＿＿　　e. 征服者
6. conqueror　　＿＿＿＿＿　　f. 装腔作势地
7. male character　　＿＿＿＿＿　　g. 中国曲艺
8. facial make-up　　＿＿＿＿＿　　h. 人物性格
9. in despair　　＿＿＿＿＿　　i. 面具
10. commit suicide　　＿＿＿＿＿　　j. 喜剧角色

Ⅱ. *Fill in the blanks according to the text.*

1. From the facial make-up, we can instantly tell ＿＿＿＿＿＿.

2. It combines music, dance, acrobatics and ＿＿＿＿＿＿.

3. They are Sheng, Dan, Jing, Chou, that is, ＿＿＿＿＿＿, female character, male character with a painted face and clown.

4. Later, ＿＿＿＿＿ replaced the mask.

5. Xiang Yu is wearing a ＿＿＿＿＿ mask.

Ⅲ. *Translate the following sentences according to the dialogue.*

1. The actors and actresses in Peking Opera all wear facial makeup that indicates their personalities.

2. The black color symbolizes firmness and honesty.

3. A white face symbolizes cruelty.

4. While black and white face shows a defeated hero who is brave, cocky and foolhardy.

5. It symbolizes loyalty and courage.

Ⅳ. *Work in pairs and discuss the following questions.*

1. How do you think of Peking Opera?
2. Have you ever watched *Farewell to My Concubine* before? Can you tell the story in English?

Knowledge Expansion

Peking Opera is a synthesis of stylized action, singing, dialogue, mime, acrobatic, fighting and dancing to represent a story or depict different characters and their feelings of gladness, anger, sorrow, happiness, surprise, fear and sadness. The characters may be loyal or treacherous, beautiful or ugly, good or bad. Their images are always vividly manifested in bright costumes that show the styles of ancient China.

Four Main Characters

There are currently four main role categories in Peking Opera. They are Sheng, Dan, Jing, Chou. Any role in these categories or sub-categories can be the leading role in a play. Except the second category—Dan, the other three categories are for male characters.

The Music of Peking Opera

The melodies have harmonious rhythms and are described as graceful and pleasing to the ears. The melody may be classified into two groups: Xipi and Erhuang. The performance is accompanied by a tune played on wind instruments, percussion instruments, and stringed instruments. The chief musical instruments are Jinghu (a two-stringed bowed instrument with a high register), Yueqin (a four-stringed plucked instrument with a full-moon-shaped sound box), Sanxian (a three-stringed plucked instrument), Suona horn, flute, drum, big-gong, cymbals, small-gong, etc.

The Costumes in Peking Opera

Often the most recognizable feature of Peking Opera, the costumes are graceful, elegant, and brilliant in color and design. They are mostly made using hand sewing and embroidery. As the traditional Chinese patterns are adopted, the costumes are of a high aesthetic value.

Facial Make-up in Peking Opera

Facial make-up and masks are very important to the aesthetic of Peking Opera. The colors are rich and depict different characters using symbolism of color. Black will often represent intelligent characters, while white indicates wickedness.

Lesson 2 Peking Opera 京剧

Peking Opera Stage Set-up

In the past, stages in most Chinese theaters were square platforms exposed to the audience on three sides. Occasionally, stages would be exposed on all four sides and would have a central platform. In the latter case, performances could be watched from the back also.

Much like the traditional stage curtains in the West, an embroidered curtain known as a Shoujiu was hung over the platform, which divided the stage into two parts: the back stage and the stage.

(Excerpted from www.bing.com)

参考译文

课文阅读

京剧是中国曲艺的传统形式。它结合了音乐、舞蹈、杂技和声乐表演。根据角色的性别、年龄、社会地位和职业，京剧中的角色一般分为四种主要类型，分别是生、旦、净、丑。京剧脸谱的历史要追溯到很久以前。在古代，演员在表演京剧时都戴着面具，后来，脸谱取代了面具。依靠脸谱，我们可以瞬间判断人物的个性。

欣赏京剧的最佳场所是梨园，其字面意思是梨园，也指戏曲表演者受训练的地方。许多京剧大师经常在这里演出。

自1919年京剧大师梅兰芳访问日本以来，京剧在世界各地越来越受欢迎，它为中西文化交流做出了杰出贡献。如今，可以在许多国际城市和当地的"唐人街"遇到京剧表演者的旅行剧团。

扩展阅读

京剧是程式化的动作、歌唱、对话、哑剧、杂技、格斗和舞蹈的合成，以表达故事或刻画不同的角色及其喜乐、愤怒、悲伤、幸福、惊奇、恐惧和悲伤。角色可能是忠诚的或奸诈的，美丽的或丑陋的，好的或坏的。他们的形象总是生动地表现在鲜艳的服装上，展现了中国古代的风格。

四个主要角色

京剧目前有四个主要角色，分别是生、旦、净、丑。这些类别或子类别中的任何角色都可以成为戏剧中的主角。除了第二类——旦，其他三个类别都是男性角色。

京剧音乐

京剧的旋律具有和谐的节奏，优美而悦耳。旋律可分为两类："西皮"和"二黄"。该演奏伴有在管乐器、打击乐器和弦乐器上演奏的曲调。主要乐器有：京胡（一种高声调的双弦弓乐器）、月琴（一种带有全月形琴体的四弦弹拨乐器）、三弦（一种三弦弹拨乐器）、唢呐、笛子、鼓、大锣、镲、小锣、钹等。

071

京剧服装

京剧服装通常是京剧最显著的特色,其色彩和设计优雅、雅致、明亮。它们大多使用手工缝制和刺绣制成。由于采用了中国传统图案,因此这些服装具有很高的美学价值。

京剧脸谱

脸谱和面具对京剧的美学起到非常重要的作用。脸谱颜色丰富,并使用颜色象征性地描绘不同的性格。黑色通常代表聪明的人物,而白色则代表邪恶。

京剧舞台布置

过去,大多数中国剧院的舞台都是方形的平台,从三个侧面向观众展示。有时,舞台所有四个侧面都暴露在外,有一个中央平台。在后一种情况下,也可以从后面观看表演。

与西方的传统舞台幕布很像,被称为"守旧"的绣花幕布悬挂在平台上,将平台分为两部分:后台和舞台。

参考答案

Exercises

Ⅰ. 1—5 g j i h f   6—10 e d c b a

Ⅱ. 1. the personalities of the characters

2. vocal performance

3. male character

4. facial make-up

5. black and white

Ⅲ. 1. 京剧中男演员和女演员都画着脸谱,以表明自己的个性。

2. 黑色脸谱象征坚定和诚实。

3. 白脸象征着残酷。

4. 黑白脸谱表现出一个勇敢、自大和顽强的被击败的英雄。

5. 它象征着忠诚和勇气。

Ⅳ. Omitted

Lesson 3 Zhusuan 珠算

Warm-Up

Work in pairs. Learn the following words and phrases. Then answer the following questions.

1. Draw a picture of an abacus, and describe its structure.
2. Can you make a brief introduction of Zhusuan?

Words and Expressions

Read the following words and expressions. Then try to memorize them.

abacus *n.* 算盘	traditional *a.* 传统；习俗的；惯例的
calculating *a.* 计算的；深谋远虑的	deck *n.* 甲板；舱面；（船或公共汽车的）层面
rod *n.* 长杆；长棒	bead *n.* （有孔的）珠子
calculation *n.* 计算	correct *a.* 准确无误的；精确的

Useful Expressions

1. I have never heard of that before.
2. It is Chinese abacus, a traditional tool for calculating.
3. How does it work?
4. The upper deck has two beads on each rod.
5. I do feel that it helps to improve my memory.
6. I hope it will work.

Dialogue

Watch the animation, then practice the dialogue by reading it aloud with your partner. Read it through at least twice, and change your role each time.

(**Scene:** Sally is a college student in Cultural and Tourism School from China. Sam is an exchange student from America. In the classroom at campus, Sally is learning Chinese abacus. Sam is very curious about it.)

Sam: Hi, Sally. What are you doing?

Sally: I am learning Zhusuan by watching a video.

Sam: Zhusuan? I have never heard of that before. What is that?

Sally: It is Chinese abacus, a traditional tool for calculating.

Sam: So how does it work?

Sally: It has two decks with more than 7 rods. The upper deck has two beads on each rod. Each bead means 5. On the lower deck, there are 5 beads on each rod and each bead means 1.

Sam: It is cool. So the beads are moved up and down during calculation?

Sally: Yes. That is correct. Do you want to have a try?

Sam: Yes. It is interesting.

Sally: In the process of learning, I do feel that it helps to improve my memory.

Sam: Really? My memory is getting bad recently. I think I have to try it then.

Sally: I hope it will work.

Questions:

1. What is Zhusuan?
2. What's the function of abacus?
3. How many beads are there on each rod for the upper deck?
4. What is Zhusuan good for?

Role-Play

Act it out according to the instructions.

A student from China: Sally

1. To greet Sam and extend welcome to him.
2. Sally tells him Chinese abacus has a long history, and explains the structure of an abacus.
3. Sally tells him many ways to improve memory.

A student from America: Sam

1. To greet Sally.
2. To show curiosity about Chinese abacus.
3. To ask how to have a good memory.

Lesson 3 Zhusuan 珠算

➡ Passage Reading

Zhusuan, known as the Chinese abacus, is an ancient calculating method with a history of over 2,500 years, and it was officially listed as an intangible cultural heritage at the 8th UNESCO World Heritage Congress. It is regarded as the fifth great invention in Chinese history and was listed as a national-level intangible cultural heritage in 2008.

The abacus has two decks and more than seven rods. The upper deck, which is known as heaven, has two beads on each rod. These beads each have the value of five. There are five beads on the bottom deck, known as earth. Each of these has the value of one. The beads are moved up and down during calculation.

The abacus's popularity has been compromised over the course of time by the emergence of digital calculators; however, they are still in use in many of China's rural marketplaces. Today, the abacus has a richer value as a cultural symbol rather than as a practical calculating tool.

Useful Words and Expressions:

ancient *a.* 古老的；古代的
intangible *a.* 触摸不到的；无形的
congress *n.* 代表大会；国会
digital calculator 数字计算器
officially *ad.* 正式地；官方地
compromise *v.* 妥协；让步
cultural heritage 文化遗产
rural marketplace 农村市场

Translation Tasks:

1. 珠算是具有 2,500 多年历史的一种古老的计算方法。
2. 这些珠子在计算过程中上下来回移动。
3. 上层，称作"天"，每个档上有两颗珠子。
4. 在第 8 届联合国世界遗产大会上，珠算正式列入非物质文化遗产。
5. These beads each have the value of five.
6. The abacus's popularity has been compromised over the course of time by the emergence of digital calculators.
7. However, they are still in use in many of China's rural marketplaces.
8. There are five beads on the bottom deck, known as earth.

➡ Exercises

Ⅰ. *Match the following words and phrases, and write the corresponding letter for each item.*

1. UNESCO   _____   a. 国家级
2. congress   _____   b. 出现

3. bottom deck   _____   c. 象征
4. intangible   _____   d. 珠子
5. symbol   _____   e. 大会
6. emergence   _____   f. 无形的
7. calculating tool   _____   g. 联合国教科文组织
8. upper deck   _____   h. 下层
9. national-level   _____   i. 计算工具
10. bead   _____   j. 上层

Ⅱ. Fill in the blanks according to the text.

1. The abacus has two decks, namely, _____.
2. On the bottom deck, there are _____ on each rod.
3. The abacus is an ancient tool for _____.
4. Learning abacus is good for _____.
5. Nowadays, the abacus owns a richer significance as _____.

Ⅲ. Translate the following sentences according to the dialogue.

1. It is Chinese abacus, a traditional tool for calculating.
2. So the beads are moved up and down during calculation?
3. My memory is getting bad recently.
4. On the lower deck, there are 5 beads on each rod and each bead means 1.
5. In the process of learning, I do feel that it helps to improve my memory.

Ⅳ. Work in pairs and discuss the following questions.

1. How do you think of the compromise for Chinese abacus?
2. If you have learnt Zhusuan before, can you talk about its influence on you?

➡ Knowledge Expansion

In 2007, the British newspaper *The Independent* listed 101 small inventions that changed the world, among which, the Chinese abacus, which has enjoyed a history of 2,000 years or so, ranked the first.

The abacus was a great invention in ancient China. The abacus was invented on the basis that Chinese used the counting-rod for a long period. In ancient times, people used small rods to count. Later, with the development of productivity, the amount requiring calculation was greater, and calculation with counting-rods limited the calculation. Thus, people invented a more advanced counter — the abacus.

Lesson 3　Zhusuan　珠算

The earliest known painting of the Chinese abacus can be found in the famous long scroll *Riverside Scene at Qingming Festival* painted by Zhang Zeduan (1085—1145) during the Song Dynasty (960—1279). There, an abacus is clearly seen lying beside an account book on the counter of an apothecary's.

The abacus is rectangular with wooden frame on the four sides and small rods fixed inside strung with wooden beads; a girder across the middle separates the abacus into two parts: each rod has two beads on its upper part, each representing five, and five beads on the lower part, each representing one.

With the application of the abacus, people summarized many abacus rhymes, increasing the calculating speed. By the time of the Ming Dynasty, people could use the abacus in addition, subtraction, multiplication and division, which were widely used in calculating weight, amount, space and volume.

Since it is simple to make an abacus and cheap to buy one, and it is easy to remember simple abacus rhymes, and convenient to calculate with an abacus, it is widely used in China. There are many experts in the use of the abacus in all trades and professions, and some people can use an abacus with two hands at the same time.

Later the abacus was gradually spread into Japan, Republic of Korea, America, and countries and regions in Southeast Asia. People find that using an abacus can improve thinking and practical abilities in addition to providing convenient calculation. Since it requires cooperation of the mind, eyes and hand, it is a good way to improve the comprehensive reaction ability.

参考译文

课文阅读

珠算，就是中国的算盘。它是具有2,500多年历史的一种古老的计算方法。在第8届联合国世界遗产大会上，珠算正式列入非物质文化遗产。在中国历史上，把珠算视为第5大发明，在2008年，将珠算列为中国非物质文化遗产。

算盘有两层，7个档以上。上层，称作"天"，每个档上有两颗珠子，每个珠子代表数字5。下层有5颗珠子，称为"地"，每个珠子表示数字1。这些珠子在计算过程中上下来回移动。

随着数字计算器的出现，算盘的受欢迎程度大大降低了。然而，在中国的农村市场中仍然在使用。如今，算盘不再作为一种实用的计算工具，而是作为一种富有更多价值的文化象征而存在。

扩展阅读

2007年，英国《独立报》评选出101款改变世界的小发明，排在第一位是有近2,000

年历史的中国算盘。

算盘是中国古代一项伟大的发明，是中国人在长期使用算筹的基础上发明的。古时候，人们用小木棍进行计算。后来，随着生产的发展，需要计算的数目越来越大，用小木棍计算受到了限制，于是，人们又发明了更先进的计算器——算盘。

最早的算盘图见北宋画家张择端（1085—1145）的《清明上河图》长卷。画卷上一家药铺柜台上账本左边，一个算盘清晰可见。

算盘是长方形的，四周是木框，里面固定一根根小木棍，小木棍上穿着木珠，中间有一根横梁把算盘分成两部分：每根木棍的上半部有两个珠子，每个珠子代表5；下半部有5个珠子，每个珠子代表1。

随着算盘的使用，人们总结出许多计算口诀，使计算的速度更快了。这种用算盘计算的方法，叫珠算。到了明代，珠算已能进行加减乘除的运算，广泛用于计算物体的重量、数量、面积、体积等。

由于算盘制作简单，价格便宜，珠算口诀便于记忆，运算又简便，所以算盘在中国被广泛使用。中国各行各业都有一批打算盘的高手，而且有的人能用左右两只手同时打算盘。

算盘后来陆续流传到了日本、韩国、美国和东南亚等国家和地区。人们在使用过程中发现，使用算盘，除了运算方便以外，还有锻炼思维能力和动手能力的作用。因为打算盘需要脑、眼、手的密切配合，是训练综合反应能力的一种好方法。

参考答案

Exercises

Ⅰ. 1—5　g e h f c　　6—10　b i j a d

Ⅱ. 1. upper deck and lower deck
2. 5 beads
3. calculating
4. improving memory
5. a cultural symbol

Ⅲ. 1. 中国的算盘是一种传统的计算工具。
2. 那么这些珠子是在计算过程中上下来回移动吗？
3. 最近我的记忆力变差了。
4. 在下层中，每根档上有5颗珠子，每颗珠子表示1。
5. 在学习过程中，我觉得我的记忆力好像提高了。

Ⅳ. Omitted

Unit VI
Chinese Cuisine

中国美食

Lesson 1   Hot Pot   火锅

Warm-Up

Work in pairs. Learn the following words and phrases. Then answer the following questions.

1. What is your favorite Chinese food? Describe its taste.
2. Name a few different styles of hot pot.
3. How often do you eat hot pot?

Words and Expressions

Read the following words and expressions. Then try to memorize them.

dip *v.* 涮，浸，蘸	bland *a.* 无滋味的；枯燥乏味的；没精打采的
seasoning *n.* 调味品，作料	sesame *n.* 芝麻
ferment *v.* 发酵	invite over 邀请（某人）来家里
hot and spicy 辛辣的	soup base 汤底
dipping sauce 蘸料	

Useful Expressions

1. Hot pot is very popular all over China.
2. There is not much flavour in it.
3. I am going to invite my friends over for dinner.
4. It tastes like heaven.
5. Eating hot pot can be a great way to socialize.
6. Hot pot is much more favoured in winter.

Dialogue

Watch the animation, then practice the dialogue by reading it aloud with your partner. Read it through at least twice, and change your role each time.

(**Scene:** Sally is a college student in Cultural and Tourism School from China. Sam is an

Lesson 1 Hot Pot 火锅

exchange student from America. Sally invites Sam over for dinner. They are going to have hot pot this evening.)

Sally: Hello Sam, how are you?
Sam: I am pretty good. How are you? Thank you for inviting me over for dinner.
Sally: Come in, it is really nice to see you. You look great!
Sam: Thanks, so do you. Well, what are you cooking? It smells so good.
Sally: I am making Chinese hot pot at home.
Sam: Really? That's so exciting! I love hot pot.
Sally: I love it too. It is getting cold lately. Hot pot is the best choice in winter.
Sam: Agreed. What soup base are we having today?
Sally: I got this little mutton soup base package from an Asian market. It is a bit spicy, but it tastes like heaven.
Sam: Yes, I see that little sheep symbol, it is actually a worldwide hot pot franchise.
Sally: I think we got the right one.
Sam: Absolutely.

Questions:

1. Is hot pot a type of healthy food?
2. Why is hot pot good to eat in winter?
3. Name a few different hot pot soup bases people usually choose.
4. Name a few seasonings you may put in your dipping sauce.
5. What can you cook in a hot pot?

➡ Role-Play

Act it out according to the instructions.

A student in China: Sally

1. Greets Sam in a casual way.
2. Asks Sam out for dinner.
3. Asks for dinner suggestions.

A student from America: Sam

1. Greets Sally in a casual way.
2. Takes Sally's invitation.
3. Agrees on hot pot with Sally.

Passage Reading

Chongqing Hot Pot

Without doubt, Chongqing could be called Chinese "hot pot capital" — it is said that five out of six restaurants in Chongqing are hot pot places. According to the Chongqing Hot Pot Association, the city has more than 20,000 hot pot restaurants which own 50,000 franchises around the country. The history of hot pot is somewhat contested, but if you'd ask people in Chongqing, hot pot originated long ago in their city, by boatmen along the Yangtze River.

The heavily flavored broth and numbing hot spiciness is what Chongqing hot pot is most known for. The hot pot soup base uses premium butter as its special ingredient, giving the broth a very rich taste that perfectly matches the red hot chili.

Amongst the many ingredients used in Chongqing hot pot, this spicy hot pot is often eaten with fresh cow stomach. For dipping sauce, sesame oil is commonly used to balance the taste of spice.

It is the Sichuan pepper that gives Chongqing its "numbing" spiciness, which makes your lips and mouth tingle a bit.

Useful Words and Expressions:

association *n.* 协会；社团；联盟	franchise *n.* 特许经营权
contest *v.* 质疑	numbing *a.* 使人麻木的
ingredient *n.* 成分，原料	broth *n.* 汤
tingle *n./v.* 刺痛	

Translation Tasks:

1. 毫无疑问，重庆可以称为中国火锅之都。
2. 据说，每六间饭店中就有五间是火锅店。
3. 火锅很久之前就起源于重庆。
4. 火锅的汤底原料使用的是高端牛油。
5. The history of hot pot is somewhat contested.
6. The heavily flavored broth and numbing hot spiciness is what Chongqing hot pot is most known for.
7. For dipping sauce, sesame oil is commonly used to balance the spice.
8. It is the Sichuan pepper that gives Chongqing its "numbing" spiciness, which makes your lips and mouth tingle a bit.

Exercises

I. *Match the following words and phrases, and write the corresponding letter for each item.*

1. numbing　　　　＿＿＿＿　　a. 刺痛
2. originate　　　　＿＿＿＿　　b. 匹配
3. match　　　　　＿＿＿＿　　c. 起源
4. balance　　　　＿＿＿＿　　d. 平衡
5. tingle　　　　　＿＿＿＿　　e. 麻木的
6. contest　　　　＿＿＿＿　　f. 质疑

II. *Fill in the blanks according to the text.*

1. Without doubt, Chongqing could be called Chinese "hot pot ＿＿＿＿".
2. The hot pot soup base uses premium butter as its special ＿＿＿＿.
3. Chongqing hot pot features its broth with a very ＿＿＿＿ taste.
4. For dipping sauce, sesame oil is commonly used to ＿＿＿＿ the spice.
5. Its "numbing" spiciness that makes your lips and mouth ＿＿＿＿ a bit.

III. *Translate the following sentences according to the dialogue.*

1. Thank you for inviting me over for dinner.
2. It smells so good.
3. I am making Chinese hot pot at home.
4. It is getting cold lately.
5. 火锅是冬天里最好的选择。
6. 今天我们用什么汤底？
7. 它有一点辣，但是超级好吃。
8. 我想我们买对了。

IV. *Work in pairs and discuss the following questions.*

1. Which hot pot soup base is your favourite?
2. In your opinion, is hot pot a healthy choice?

Knowledge Expansion

Hot pot is all about relaxing and freedom to eat, but there is some etiquette one should keep in mind. Avid food lover the Wanderluster explains Chinese hot pot etiquette, and shares some do's and don'ts.

As a loyal fan of hot pot, I've frequented countless hot pot places in various countries and often make it at home too. I have hot pot so often, that I've established a set of hot pot etiquette rules, much to the pain of my fellow diners, including my dad. Here we go:

1. Don't mix the utensils.

The list of hot pot ingredients is endless, and many of them are raw meats or fish.

Whenever dealing with raw food, it is important one does not use the same chopsticks for putting the raw food in the pot and also for eating. So remember that separate utensils should be used for dining and handling of raw ingredients.

2. No plastic please.

With soup hot enough to cook raw meat, please don't dip any plastic or non-heat-safe utensils in the hot pot. My dad did exactly that with a pair of plastic chopsticks while I looked on in horror, screaming "It's plastic!" with my mouth full of noodles. You really don't want anything inorganic dissolving into the soup.

3. Take time to enjoy.

A hot pot meal takes time, especially when there are so many hot pot ingredients on the table. Each hot pot ingredient is meant to be savoured slowly. If you are in a rush, please reschedule the meal.

Cook each piece of meat, seafood, mushroom or vegetable as you eat. An exception is made for ingredients that require a longer cooking time such as potato, winter melon, and radish.

4. Cook each hot pot ingredient as it's meant to be cooked.

A good way to cook thinly sliced meat is to deploy the "seven up eight down" method, which metaphorically refers to the palpitations of a worried or anxious heart in a Chinese saying. Simply dip the meat in and out of the boiling soup eight times and it should be nicely cooked.

While most meat and seafood cook well in all sorts of soup base, soup-absorbing ingredients like vegetables, mushrooms and soy products fare better in non-spicy soup base.

5. Stop refilling the stock until I say so!

The best part of the hotpot for me is the soup. After absorbing all the wonderful flavours of the meat, seafood, mushrooms and vegetables, the soup makes a precious bowl of elixir and nothing infuriates me more than seeing someone refill the soup without asking, and diluting all the flavours.

Very often, as the service staff approach with the soup kettle, I put up the emergency stop sign and unabashedly scoop a few bowls of soup on standby before allowing the refill.

参考译文

课文阅读

重庆火锅

毫无疑问,重庆可被称为中国火锅之都。据说,每六间饭店就有五间是火锅店。基于重庆火锅协会的数据,重庆有两万多家火锅店,在全国有多达五万家加盟店。火锅的历史至今还有争议,但是在重庆人看来,火锅很久之前就起源于重庆,由扬子江边的船夫们发明。

重庆火锅以重口味和麻辣闻名。汤底以高端牛油为原料,带来厚重的味道,是辣椒的绝配。

重庆火锅最常见的食材就是毛肚。说到蘸料,芝麻油通常拿来中和辛辣。

四川的麻椒使重庆火锅带给你的舌头和嘴一点发麻的感觉。

扩展阅读

吃火锅就是要放松自己,大饱口福,但是有一些礼仪需要牢记。狂热的美食爱好者 Wanderluster 讲解了中国的火锅礼仪,并分享了一些可做和不可做的事情。

作为火锅的忠实粉丝,我经常光顾各个国家的许多火锅店,也经常在家里自制火锅。我经常吃火锅,于是制订了一套吃火锅的礼仪,这给包括我父亲在内的同伴们带来了很多困扰。具体如下:

1. 不要混用餐具

火锅配料种类繁多,其中许多是生肉或鱼。每当处理生鲜食材时,重要的是不要使用相同的筷子将生食放入锅中并用这双筷子进食。因此,请记住,应使用单独的餐具来用餐和处理食材。

2. 请不要用任何塑料制品

汤热得足以煮生肉时,请不要在火锅中浸入任何塑料制品或不耐热的器具。我父亲就真的用过塑料筷子,那时我嘴巴里塞满面条,惊恐地看着一副塑料筷子,尖叫道:"那是塑料的!"不要让任何无机物溶解到汤中。

3. 花时间享受

吃一顿火锅要花一些时间,尤其是当桌上有那么多火锅食材时。每种火锅配料都应慢慢品尝。如果赶时间,请重新安排用餐时间。

边吃边煮每块肉、海鲜、蘑菇或蔬菜。对于需要较长烹饪时间的食材(如土豆、冬瓜和萝卜)则是例外。

4. 正确地涮煮每一种火锅食材

涮煮被切成薄片的肉的一种好方法是采用"七上八下"的方法,"七上八下"在中文里暗指担心或焦虑导致的心脏跳动。只需将肉浸入沸腾的汤中八次,应该就可煮熟。

虽然大多数肉类和海鲜类适合各种汤底,但是吸收汤汁的食材(如蔬菜、蘑菇和豆制品)更适合不辣的汤底。

5. 在食客同意之前别加汤

对我来说,火锅最好的部分是汤。吸收了肉、海鲜、蘑菇和蔬菜的所有奇妙风味后,汤变成一碗珍贵的"灵丹妙药"。有人连问都不问就在火锅里加汤,稀释掉汤的味道,会让人感到恼火。

很多时候,当服务人员拿着汤壶前来时,我会马上叫停,在同意加汤之前,毫不犹豫地盛几碗汤来备用。

参考答案

Exercises

Ⅰ. 1-6　e c b d a f

Ⅱ. 1. capital

　 2. ingredient

　 3. rich

　 4. balance

　 5. tingle

Ⅲ. 1. 谢谢邀请我来你家吃晚饭。

　 2. 闻起来真香。

　 3. 我在家做火锅。

　 4. 最近天气转冷了。

　 5. Hot pot is the best choice in winter.

　 6. What soup base are we having today?

　 7. It is a bit spicy, but it tastes like heaven.

　 8. I think we got the right one.

Ⅳ. Omitted

Lesson 2   Peking Duck   北京烤鸭

Warm-Up

Work in pairs. Learn the following words and phrases. Then answer the following questions.

1. Have you ever eaten Peking duck? Do you enjoy it?
2. What is so special about Peking duck?
3. Is Peking duck a healthy food?

Words and Expressions

Read the following words and expressions. Then try to memorize them.

cuisine *n.* 饭菜，菜肴	imperial *a.* 帝国的，皇帝的
feast *n.* 盛宴，宴会	authentic *a.* 真正的，真品的
slice *v.* 把……切成（薄）片	pancake *n.* 烙饼，薄饼
spread over 分散，分开	a deep impression 深刻的印象
roll up 卷起来	

Useful Expressions

1. This is no doubt that Peking duck is a world-famous dish of Beijing.
2. Peking duck is now considered a national dish of China and truly has become an important part of Chinese tradition.
3. When treating somebody with Peking duck, it seems that it is a feast for a VIP.
4. Peking duck should traditionally be eaten entirely and sliced in front of the diners by the cook.
5. The crispy skin and the juicy meat leave a deep impression on first-time consumers during their Beijing trip.
6. Tasting Peking duck is one of the must-do things in a Beijing tour.

Dialogue

Watch the animation, then practice the dialogue by reading it aloud with your partner.

Read it through at least twice, and change your role each time.

(**Scene:** Sally is a college student in Cultural and Tourism School from China. Sam is an exchange student from America. Sally tells Sam that Peking duck is a great choice for tourists.)

Sally: Hi, Sam, what's happening?

Sam: Not much, Sally, my sister Lisa's coming to Beijing this week, I'm pretty excited.

Sally: Cool. Are you planning to stay at home and catch up or are you going to the downtown area?

Sam: Well, actually, I want to show her around.

Sally: Do you want to eat Peking duck?

Sam: Peking duck?

Sally: Yeah, Peking duck is a dish that many tourists want to try in Beijing. Here I got a gift voucher for a restaurant named Huajiayiyuan right here near the district. I'd be happy to give them to you.

Sam: Wow, that's very nice of you.

Sally: The restaurant is located in a Siheyuan, a traditional Chinese building.

Sam: Well, I think I know the place you are talking about. The food critics give it a very high rating.

Sally: Yeah, the Peking duck there is low-fat. Remember you'll have to make reservations beforehand. I am sure your sister will have a great time there.

Sam: Ha, perfect!

Questions:

1. What kind of duck is Peking duck?
2. Why is peking duck popular in China?
3. How is Peking duck eaten?
4. Why is Peking duck so expensive?

Role-Play

Act it out according to the instructions.

A student in China: Sally

1. Greets Sam in a casual way.
2. Recommends Peking duck.
3. Offers a gift voucher.

Lesson 2　Peking Duck　北京烤鸭

A student from America: Sam

1. Greets Sally in a casual way.
2. Tells Sally that his sister Lisa is coming to visit him this week.
3. Asks where to have the authentic local food.

Passage Reading

Eating Peking duck in Beijing is something you've got to add to your bucket list! I had seen plenty of bright red ducks hanging in the shop windows in San Francisco's Chinatown, but I had no idea what the actual dining process was like until I sat down for the traditional meal at a Chinese restaurant. The roast duck is hand-cut in thin slices in front of you. It's served with cucumber, spring onion, a sweet brown sauce, and thin crepes. Everything is served in separate dishes, so you can customize your own little burrito-like things and enjoy! The veggies are bright, the duck meat is tender with crispy skin, and the thick sauce is both sweet and savory. It's a delicious combination of traditional Chinese textures and flavors.

Useful Words and Expressions:

bucket list 目标清单	hand-cut 手工切割
crepe 薄饼	burrito 墨西哥玉米饼
savory 美味的，可口的	

Translation Tasks:

1. 在北京吃北京烤鸭是你必须加在你的清单上的事情！
2. 我看到很多鲜红色的鸭子挂在商店的橱窗里。
3. 我不知道实际的用餐过程是什么样的。
4. The roast duck is hand-cut in thin slices in front of you..
5. Everything is served in separate dishes, so you can customize your own little burrito-like things and enjoy!
6. It's a delicious combination of traditional Chinese textures and flavors.
7. If you're looking for restaurant recommendations I can suggest those with certainty!

Exercises

Ⅰ. *Match the following words and phrases, and write the corresponding letter for each item.*

1. hang　　　_____　　a. 用餐
2. satisfy　　_____　　b. 服务

3. serve　　　　　_____　　c. 满意

4. dine　　　　　 _____　　d. 悬挂

5. customize　　 _____　　e. 定制

6. explode　　　 _____　　f. 爆炸

Ⅱ. *Fill in the blanks according to the text.*

1. Eating Peking duck in Beijing is something you've got to add to _____.

2. The roast duck is hand-cut in _____ in front of you.

3. Diners wrap the slices in a _____.

4. The duck slices are brought to the table with garnishes and sauce including _____.

5. The duck meat is _____.

Ⅲ. *Translate the following sentences according to the dialogue.*

1. My sister Lisa's coming to Beijing this week, I'm pretty excited.

2. I want to show her around.

3. Peking duck is a dish that many tourists want to try in Beijing.

4. I'd be happy to give them to you.

5. 我这里有一张餐馆的礼券。

6. 餐厅位于一个四合院中，四合院是一种中国传统建筑。

7. 美食评论家给了它很高的评价。

8. 你得提前预订。

Ⅳ. *Work in pairs and discuss the following questions.*

1. How is Peking duck cooked?

2. Why is Peking duck special?

🡪 Knowledge Expansion

Peking duck is an iconic Beijing dish, consisting of thin pieces of tender, roasted duck meat and crispy skin wrapped in a thin crepe, along with sliced spring onions, cucumbers, and hoisin sauce or sweet bean sauce.

Evidence of preparing roasted duck in China goes as far back as the Southern and Northern Dynasties (420—589). However, it wasn't until the Yuan Dynasty (1271—1368) that the dish's association with the imperial court was first recorded, in the form of a 1330 cookbook by a royal dietary physician by the name of Hu Sihui. Hu's recipe called for a rather elaborate preparation, where the duck was roasted inside the stomach of a sheep.

Lesson 2 Peking Duck 北京烤鸭

Interestingly, although Peking duck is named after Beijing ("Peking" is an older spelling), it originated in the former Chinese capital of Nanjing, which lies in the eastern province of Jiangsu. In the Ming Dynasty, the imperial court moved to Beijing, bringing roasted duck along with it. By then, Peking duck was an established staple of imperial menus. In the Qing Dynasty, Peking duck spread to the nobility, where the dish was much praised in the writings of scholars and poets.

Even today, Peking duck retains its majestic connotations because of its specific and lengthy preparation. First, white-feathered ducks are raised in a free-range environment for 45 days, after which they are force-fed for 15 to 20 days. Once slaughtered, plucked, gutted, washed, and boiled, air is pumped under the skin so that it separates from the fat. Next, the duck is hung to dry and coated with maltose syrup to make the skin extra crispy.

It is then roasted in one of two ways: the traditional closed oven method, or the hung oven method developed in the 1860s. The two most notable Peking duck restaurants in Beijing represent the two different roasting traditions — which one is superior is a matter of great dispute. The renowned Bianyifang restaurant, which opened in the 15th century, uses the closed oven method, in which the duck is cooked by the heat radiating from the oven's walls. Meanwhile, Quanjude restaurant uses the hung oven technique invented by its founder, Yang Quanren. In this method, the duck is hung from a hook attached to the ceiling and roasted over burning wood.

In addition to its rich heritage, Peking duck has played a prominent role in Chinese international relations through the 20th and 21st centuries. Political leaders and diplomats such as Henry Kissinger, Richard Nixon, and Fidel Castro have all been famously wined and dined with this famous Chinese dish.

参考译文

课文阅读

在北京吃烤鸭是你必须加在你的清单上的事情！在旧金山唐人街，我看到很多鲜红色的鸭子挂在商店的橱窗里，但是直到我在一家中国餐馆吃到真正传统的中华料理，我才知道实际的就餐过程是什么样的。烤鸭是在你面前手工切成薄片的。这道菜搭配有黄瓜、大葱、甜面酱和薄饼。每一种配料都是分开提供的，所以你可以定制自己喜欢的小煎饼！蔬菜鲜亮，鸭肉软嫩，鸭皮酥脆，酱汁浓甜可口，这是一种传统中国味道和口感相辅相成的结合。

扩展阅读

北京烤鸭是一道标志性的北京菜，由细嫩的烤鸭肉和外皮酥脆的薄饼，以及切成片的葱、黄瓜和海鲜酱或甜面酱组成。

烤鸭制作可以追溯到南北朝（420—589）时期。然而，直到元代（1271—1368），烤鸭和朝廷的联系才第一次被记录下来，忽思慧于1330年所撰《饮膳正要》中有所记载。他的食谱要求精心准备并在羊肚子里烤鸭子。

有趣的是，虽然北京烤鸭是以北京命名的（"Peking"是旧时拼写），但它起源于中国前首都南京，位于中国东部省份江苏省。明朝时，朝廷迁往北京，烤鸭也随之被带往北京。那时，北京烤鸭已经成为宫廷菜单上的主食。到了清代，北京烤鸭传到了贵族阶层，北京烤鸭在学者和诗人的作品中广受赞誉。

即使在今天，北京烤鸭仍然保留着其宏伟的内涵，源于它精心而漫长的准备。首先，将白羽鸭在自由放养的环境中饲养45天，然后强制喂养15至20天。一旦屠宰，就退毛、去内脏、清洗、沸煮、空气被泵入皮肤下，使其与脂肪分离。接下来，将鸭肉晾干，涂上麦芽糖浆，可使鸭皮格外酥脆。

烤鸭的方法有两种：一种是传统的焖炉烤鸭，另一种是19世纪60年代发展起来的挂炉烤鸭。北京最著名的两家烤鸭店代表了两种不同的烤鸭传统——哪一种烤鸭更优是一个具有很大争议的问题。著名的便宜坊餐厅，开业于15世纪，采用焖炉法，烤鸭是靠烤箱壁散发的热量来烹调的。同时，全聚德餐厅采用其创始人杨全仁发明的挂炉技术。这种方法是把鸭子挂在钩子上，在燃烧的木头上烤。

北京烤鸭不仅是丰富的文化遗产，在20世纪和21世纪的中国国际关系中也起到非常重要的作用。基辛格、尼克松和卡斯特罗等政界领袖和外交官都曾享用这道中国名菜，配美酒佳肴一起享用。

参考答案

Exercises

Ⅰ. 1—6 d c b a e f

Ⅱ. 1. bucket list

   2. thin slices

   3. crepe

   4. cucumber, spring onion, a sweet brown sauce, and thin crepes

   5. tender with crispy skin

Ⅲ. 1. 我妹妹丽萨这周要来北京，我很兴奋。

   2. 我想带她四处看看。

3. 北京烤鸭是很多游客想在北京品尝的一道菜。

4. 我很乐意把它们给你。

5. Here I got a gift voucher for a restaurant.

6. The restaurant is located in a Siheyuan, a traditional Chinese building.

7. The food critics gave it a very high rating.

8. You'll have to make reservations beforehand.

Ⅳ. Omitted

Unit VII
Chinese Holidays
中国节日

Lesson 1　The Spring Festival　春节

Warm-Up

Work in pairs. Learn the following words and phrases. Then answer the following questions.

1. What is the most important traditional Chinese holiday?
2. Do you know the customs of the Spring Festival?
3. Why do people paste Spring Festival couplets?

Words and Expressions

Read the following words and expressions. Then try to memorize them.

happen *v.* 发生；出现	pretty *ad.* 相当；十分；非常；极；很 *a.* 漂亮的；美观的；精致的
couplet *n.* 对联；对句	reversed *adj.* 颠倒的；相反的
draw near 临近	show sb. around 带某人参观
lunar new year 农历新年	Spring Festival couplets 春联
horizontal scroll 横批	upper scroll 上联
lower scroll 下联	

Useful Expressions

1. The lunar new year is drawing near.
2. Are you thinking of joining our new year couplet club?
3. During the lunar new year, every family pastes the Spring Festival couplets on their doors.
4. Pasting couplets expresses people's delight in the festival and wishes for a better life in the coming years.
5. It sounds interesting.
6. I'll have a great time, too!

Dialogue

Watch the animation, then practice the dialogue by reading it aloud with your partner.

Lesson 1　The Spring Festival　春节

Read it through at least twice, and change your role each time.

(**Scene:** Sally is a college student in Cultural and Tourism School from China. Sam is an exchange student from America. On the playground at campus, they are having a short talk about the Spring Festival.)

Sally: Hi Sam, what happened?

Sam: Nothing. Sally, my friend's coming to Beijing this week, I'm pretty excited.

Sally: Is she going to stay for a while?

Sam: Well, she's not staying for very long. I really want to show her around.

Sally: The lunar new year is drawing near. Are you thinking of joining our new year couplet club?

Sam: New year couplet? What's that?

Sally: I mean the Spring Festival couplets. During the lunar new year, every family pastes the Spring Festival couplets on their doors.

Sam: Wow, that's pretty nice! Is it an important part of the Spring Festival culture?

Sally: Absolutely. Pasting couplets expresses people's delight in the festival and wishes for a better life in the coming years.

Sam: How to read the couplets?

Sally: First, look at the horizontal scroll. If the four characters are written from left to right, the upper scroll will be on the left, and the lower scroll on the right. If the characters of the horizontal scroll are reversed, the two side scrolls should be read from right to left.

Sam: Wow, it sounds interesting.

Sally: Yeah, your friend will have a great time.

Sam: I'll have a great time, too! I can't wait!

Questions:

1. What does "new year couplet club" mean?
2. Why do people paste the Spring Festival couplets during the lunar new year?
3. How to read the Spring Festival couplets?
4. If your foreign friend comes to China during the Spring Festival, what will you suggest your friend do to enjoy the Spring Festival?

Role-Play

Act it out according to the instructions.

A student in China: Sally

1. Greets Sam and asks about his plan for the Spring Festival.
2. Introduces the Spring Festival couplets customs.
3. Tells Sam how to read the Spring Festival couplets.

A student from America: Sam

1. Greets Sally.
2. Asks about the Spring Festival culture.
3. Tells Sally a Spring Festival couplet you know and discusses the meaning with Sally.

Passage Reading

Chinese New Year, known as the Spring Festival, is the most important traditional Chinese holiday. Chinese people celebrate it from Chinese New Year's Eve, the last day of the last month of the lunar calendar to the Lantern Festival on the 15th day of the first month of the new year. Customs and traditions concerning the celebration of the Chinese New Year vary widely from place to place. However, New Year's Eve is usually an occasion for Chinese families to gather for the annual reunion dinner. Other activities include setting off firecrackers, giving money in red envelopes, and visiting relatives and friends.

Useful Words and Expressions:

celebrate *v.* 庆祝；庆贺	eve *n.* 前夜，前夕
lunar calendar 农历	the Lantern Festival 元宵节
concern *v.* 与……有关；涉及	occasion *n.* 场合；时机
annual *a.* 年度的；每年的	reunion *v.* 重聚；团圆
set off firecrackers 放鞭炮	

Translation Tasks:

1. 中国新年是中国最重要的传统节日，也被称为春节。
2. 新年的庆祝活动从除夕开始一直延续到元宵节。
3. 每个家庭都会在除夕夜团聚，一起吃年夜饭。

Lesson 1　The Spring Festival　春节

4. 春节的其他活动还有放鞭炮、发红包和走亲访友等。

5. Customs and traditions concerning the celebration of the Chinese New Year vary widely from place to place.

6. The actual date of the Spring Festival is not a fixed date, instead it changes according to the Chinese lunar calendar every year.

7. People visit their close relatives and best friends, exchanging greetings and presents, which is known as the "New Year's Visit".

➡ Exercises

Ⅰ. *Match the following words and phrases, and write the corresponding letter for each item.*

1. happen　　　_____　　a. 带某人参观
2. reversed　　_____　　b. 水平的；与地面平行的；横的
3. show sb. around　_____　c. 对联；对句
4. horizontal　_____　　d. 农历新年
5. couplet　　_____　　e. 发生；出现
6. lunar new year　_____　f. 颠倒的；相反的

Ⅱ. *Fill in the blanks according to the text.*

1. During the lunar new year, every family pastes the _____ on their doors.
2. Pasting the couplets expresses people's _____ in the festival and _____ for a better life in the coming years.
3. Sally, my friend's coming to Beijing this week, I'm _____ excited.
4. The lunar new year is _____ near. Are you thinking of _____ our new year couplet club?
5. First, look at the _____. If the four characters are written from left to right, the _____ will be on the left, and the _____ on the right.

Ⅲ. *Translate the following sentences according to the dialogue.*

1. My friend is coming to Beijing this week, I'm pretty excited.
2. Well, she's not staying for very long. I really want to show her around.
3. The lunar new year is drawing near.
4. Your friend will have a great time.
5. Are you thinking of joining our new year couplet club?
6. 春节期间，家家户户都会在门上贴春联。

7. 贴春联表达了人们对节日的喜悦和对未来美好生活的祝愿。

8. 读春联时先看横批。如果这四个字是从左往右写的，上联在左，下联在右。

Ⅳ. **Work in pairs and discuss the following questions.**

1. Is there any special customs of the Spring Festival in the place where you live?
2. Do you know any other country's festivals and their customs?

Knowledge Expansion

The origin of the Spring Festival now is too old to be traced. It is widely believed that the word "Nian" (in Chinese means "year"), was first the name of a monster that started to prey on human beings at the night before the beginning of a new year. It had a very big mouth that would swallow many people with one bite. People were very scared. One day, an old man came to their rescue, offering to subdue "Nian". He said to "Nian" that "I hear that you are quite capable, but can you swallow other beasts on earth instead of people who are by no means your worthy opponents?" Hence, "Nian" did swallow many of the beasts of prey on earth that also harassed people and their domestic animals from time to time. After that, the old man who turned out to be an immortal fairy disappeared riding the beast "Nian". Now that "Nian" had gone and other beasts of prey are scared off into the forests, people began to enjoy their life in peace and happiness. Before the old man left, he had told the people to put up red paper decorations on their windows and doors at each year's end to scare away "Nian" in case it sneaked back again, because red is the color that the monster feared most.

From then on, the tradition of observing the conquest of "Nian" is carried on from generation to generation. The term "Guo Nian", which may mean "Survive the Nian" becomes today's "Celebrate the New Year", as the word "Guo" in Chinese having both the meaning of "passover" and "observe". The custom of putting up red paper and firing firecrackers to scare away "Nian" has been well preserved.

参考译文

课文阅读

中国新年是中国最重要的传统节日，也被称为春节。新年的庆祝活动从除夕开始一直延续到元宵节，即从农历最后一个月的最后一天至新年第一个月的第十五天。各地欢度春节的习俗和传统有很大差异，但通常每个家庭都会在除夕夜团聚，一起吃年夜饭。其他的活动还有放鞭炮、发红包和走亲访友等。

Lesson 1　The Spring Festival　春节

扩展阅读

春节的起源比较古老，无法追溯。人们普遍认为，"年"（中文的意思是"年"）是一种怪兽的名字，它在新年开始的前一天晚上开始捕食人类。它有一张大嘴巴，一口就能吞下许多人。人们非常害怕。一天，一位老人来救人们，提出要制服"年"。他对"年"说："我听说你很能干，但是你能吞下地球上其他的野兽，而不是那些根本不是你的对手的人类吗？"自此，"年"确实吞下了地球上的许多猛兽，这些猛兽曾不时地骚扰人类和他们的家畜。原来，这位老人是神仙。老人骑着野兽"年"消失了。因为"年"已经走了，其他的猛兽也被吓跑去了森林，人们开始享受和平和幸福的生活。在老人离开之前，他曾告诉人们每年年底都要在门窗上挂上红色的纸进行装饰，以吓跑"年"，以防它再溜回来，因为红色是野兽最害怕的颜色。

从此，过"年"的传统一代一代地传承下来。"过年"一词的意思从"熬过年关"变成了今天的"庆祝新年"，因为"过"在汉语中既有"过去"的意思，也有"过、举行"的意思。贴红纸、放鞭炮吓跑"年"的习俗被很好地保存了下来。

参考答案

Exercises

Ⅰ. 1—5　e f a b c d

Ⅱ. 1. Spring Festival couplets

2. delight; wishes

3. pretty

4. drawing; joining

5. horizontal scroll; upper scroll; lower scroll

Ⅲ. 1. 我朋友这星期要来北京，我很激动。

2. 她不会待太久的。我很想带她四处逛逛。

3. 农历新年快到了。

4. 你的朋友会玩得很开心。

5. 你想参加我们的春节对联俱乐部吗？

6. During the lunar new year, every family pastes the Spring Festival couplets on their doors.

7. Pasting couplets expresses people's delight in the festival and wishes for a better life in the coming years.

8. First, look at the horizontal scroll. If the four characters are written from left to right, the upper scroll will be on the left, and the lower scroll on the right.

Ⅳ. Omitted

Lesson 2　The Dragon Boat Festival　端午节

Warm-Up

Work in pairs. Learn the following words and phrases. Then answer the following questions.

1. Why do we celebrate the Dragon Boat Festival?
2. How long does the Dragon Boat Festival last?
3. What do they eat at the Dragon Boat Festival?

➡ Words and Expressions

Read the following words and expressions. Then try to memorize them.

celebrate *v.* 庆祝	commemorate *v.* 纪念
sacrifice *v.* 牺牲	patriotic *a.* 爱国的
decorate *v.* 装饰，装点	glutinous *a.* 黏的；胶质的
prevent from 防止	pyramid-shaped 金字塔形的
lunar calendar 阴历	

➡ Useful Expressions

1. The Dragon Boat Festival is celebrated every year on the fifth day of the fifth lunar month.
2. The Dragon Boat Festival is a traditional holiday to commemorate the death of the famous Chinese poet Qu Yuan.
3. Dragon boat racing and eating Zongzi are the central customs of the festival.
4. Many places in China hold dragon boat races during the festival.
5. Zongzi is a kind of sticky rice dumpling made of glutinous rice filled with meats, beans, and other fillings.
6. The flavors of Zongzi are usually different from one region to another across China.

➡ Dialogue

Watch the animation, then practice the dialogue by reading it aloud with your partner.

Lesson 2　The Dragon Boat Festival　端午节

Read it through at least twice, and change your role each time.

(**Scene:** Sally is a college student in Cultural and Tourism School from China. Sam is an exchange student from America. Sally and Sam are talking about the Dragon Boat Festival. Sally is telling the story behind the festival.)

Sally: Hey Sam, the Dragon Boat Festival is coming, do you know that?

Sam: Wow, that's cool. It would be very nice if we could have a couple of days off.

Sally: Yeah, we'll have three days off for sure.

Sam: You're right, it falls on 7th June this year and we will go back to school on the 10th.

Sally: Do you know why the holiday is celebrated?

Sam: Nope, do you?

Sally: Well, the most popular origin is closely related to the great poet Qu Yuan. He was a patriotic poet who wrote a lot of works to show his care and devotion to his country. Because of the misdeeds of jealous rivals, he eventually fell into disfavor in the emperor's court. Unable to regain the respect of the emperor, in his sorrow Qu Yuan threw himself into the Miluo River. After his death, the people crowded to the bank of the river to pay their respects to him. The fishermen sailed their boats up and down the river to look for his body. People threw Zongzi into the water to divert fish from attacking his body.

Sam: That is really a story ends in tragedy.

Sally: Yes. Once I went more deep into his whole life story, I felt extremely sad and sorry for him.

Questions:

1. Why does the date of the Dragon Boat Festival vary each year?
2. How many days off do people get during the holiday?
3. Why is the holiday celebrated?
4. Why did people throw Zongzi into water?

➡ Role-Play

Act it out according to the instructions.

A student in China: Sally

1. Greets Sam in a casual way.

2. Tells Sam a holiday is around the corner.
3. Tells Sam the story behind the holiday.

A student from America: Sam

1. Greets Sally in a casual way.
2. Confirms the date of the holiday.
3. Gives comments on the story told by Sally.

Passage Reading

Over time, both the rowing of boats and eating Zongzi became much bigger than just a simple tradition and it developed into the Dragon Boat Festival. It falls on the fifth day of the fifth lunar month. Because of this, it's also known as Double Fifth. In China, the festival is called Duanwu, literally: the "Solar Maximus festival". In the Chinese lunar calendar, Duanwu is the time when the sun is at its maximum strength. In China, the sun is considered male, as is the dragon, so the festival is held when the sun is at its peak.

In 2005, the Chinese government started a reform of its holiday system, adding three traditional holidays to the list. The Dragon Boat Festival was celebrated as a public holiday for the first time in 2008, along with the Tomb-Sweeping Day and the Mid-Autumn Festival.

Dragon boat racing and eating Zongzi are the most popular traditions at the Dragon Boat Festival. And thanks to the great Chinese diaspora, Zongzi has become just as ubiquitous around the world as the dragon boats. Today you can get sticky rice balls wrapped in pandan leaves anywhere there's a Chinese population.

Useful Words and Expressions:

lunar *a.* 月亮的，月球的	solar *a.* 太阳的，太阳能的
reform *v.* 改革，改进	diaspora *n.* 流散，移居
ubiquitous *a.* 似乎无所不在的，十分普遍的	wrap *v.* 包裹

Translation Tasks:

1. 久而久之，划船和吃粽子已经不仅仅是个习俗了，他们深深地植入到了端午节之中。
2. 端午节的日期是农历五月初五。
3. 在中国的农历里，端午节是太阳达到最大强度的时候。
4. 2005年，中国政府开始对假日制度进行改革。

5. Duanwu was celebrated as a public holiday for the first time in 2008.
6. Dragon boat racing and eating Zongzi are the most popular traditions at the Dragon Boat Festival.
7. Thanks to the great Chinese diaspora, Zongzi has become just as ubiquitous around the world as the dragon boats.
8. Today you can get sticky rice balls wrapped in pandan leaves anywhere there's a Chinese population.

Exercises

I. *Match the following words and phrases, and write the corresponding letter for each item.*

1. solar _____   a. 强度
2. strength _____   b. 月亮的
3. lunar _____   c. 发展
4. develop _____   d. 改革
5. peak _____   e. 顶点
6. reform _____   f. 太阳的

II. *Fill in the blanks according to the text.*

1. The Dragon Boat Festival falls on the fifth day of the fifth _____.
2. This is the time of year when the sun is at it's _____ strength..
3. Duanwu was celebrated as a public holiday for the first time in 2008, along with _____.
4. The most popular traditions at the Dragon Boat Festival are _____ and _____.
5. Zongzi is a _____ with fillings.

III. *Translate the following sentences according to the dialogue.*

1. The Dragon Boat Festival is coming.
2. It would be very nice if we could have a couple of days off.
3. It falls on 7th June this year and we will go back to school on the 10th.
4. The most popular origin is closely related to the great poet Qu Yuan.
5. 他是一位爱国诗人，写了许多作品来表达他对祖国的关心和奉献。
6. 屈原悲伤地跳进了汨罗江。
7. 那真是一个以悲剧结尾的故事。

8. 当我更深入地了解他的整个人生故事时，我为他感到极度的悲伤和遗憾。

Ⅳ. *Work in pairs and discuss the following questions.*

1. Why is the Dragon Boat Festival also called Duanwu?
2. Are there any countries celebrate the Dragon Boat Festival besides China?

Knowledge Expansion

Zongzi is a popular food nationwide in China, but the flavors, shapes, fillings and cooking methods vary a lot in different regions. In general, the northern ones have a sweet flavor with vegetables, dried fruits and nuts as fillings, while the southern ones are likely fat and salted with different kinds of meat as stuffing.

Cantonese Style

Zongzi in Canton is the representative style of southern China, and most of them are in pyramid shape, smaller than the ones in northern areas. The fillings of fresh meat, red bean paste and egg yolk are popular. There is also an assorted type with a mixture of diced chicken, duck, pork, mushroom or green beans.

Fujian Style

Braised pork and soda water Zongzi are the two most popular ones in Xiamen and Quanzhou, the major cities of Fujian. The former one usually uses braised pork, mushroom and shrimp and lotus seeds as extra fillings. The latter one's making procedure is much simpler. Put the soda water in the rice bundles and steam them thoroughly, which makes them taste softer and smoother.

Jiaxing Style

Jiaxing Zongzi is sought-after during the Dragon Boat Festival. In a triangular pyramid shape, the most commonly seen ones have sweet bean paste, fresh meat, lotus seed, longan and peanut. The difference is that some fat meat will be mixed in the fillings, so that it will look brilliant yellow with oil cooked out of the pork after a couple of hours' boiling and tastes of fat but not greasy.

Beijing Style

As the representative of northern Zongzi, Beijing Zongzi is smaller compared to the ones in southern areas. The bundles are usually in a pyramid shape, and the fillings are usually beans, dates and lotus seeds. Meat is seldom used as an ingredient, so most of them have a sweet flavor.

Lesson 2   The Dragon Boat Festival   端午节

Shanghai Style

With a strong flavor, Shanghai Zongzi have a great variety of ingredients, such as fresh meat, mushroom, chestnut, yolk, roast duck and red beans. The vegetarian ones sold by the Godly Restaurant are quite nice, providing wide selections like mushroom Zongzi, sweet bean paste Zongzi and pine nut rice Zongzi. Besides, Shendacheng always invents the most unique tastes and flavors, such as curry chicken Zongzi.

Taiwan Style

Taiwanese Zongzi has a flavor similar to the Fujian ones. The two most popular styles are Chengjia Meat Zongzi and Eight-ingredients Zongzi. Local people are used to making Zongzi with different kinds of meat and seafood, so most of them have a salty and sweet taste.

参考译文

课文阅读

久而久之,划船和吃粽子已经不仅仅是个习俗了,它们深深地植入到了端午节之中。端午节在农历五月初五。因此,它也被称为双五。在中国,这个节日被称为端午节,字面意思是:太阳节。在中国农历中,端午是太阳达到最大强度的时候。在中国,太阳和龙一样被认为是男性,所以这个节日是在太阳最旺盛的时候举行的。

2005年,中国政府开始对假日制度进行改革,将三个传统假日列入其中。2008年端午节第一次被列为公共节日,同时一起被列入的还有清明节和中秋节。

赛龙舟和吃粽子是端午节最受欢迎的传统活动。多亏了伟大的华人华侨,粽子在世界各地变得和龙舟一样无处不在。今天你可以在世界上任何有中国人的地方买到用斑兰叶包着的糯米球。

扩展阅读

粽子在中国是一种很受欢迎的食品,但是不同地区粽子的口味、形状、馅料和烹调方法都不尽相同。一般来说,北方地区的粽子口味是甜的,以蔬菜、干果和坚果为馅料,而南方地区钟爱各种腌制肉馅粽子。

粤式风味

广州粽子是我国南方地区具有代表性风味的粽子,而且大多呈金字塔形,比北方地区的粽子小。鲜肉、红豆酱和蛋黄的馅料很受欢迎。还有一种是鸡丁、鸭肉、猪肉、蘑菇或绿豆的混合物。

闽式风味

烧肉粽子和碱水粽子是福建省主要城市厦门和泉州的最受欢迎的两种粽子。前者通常用红烧猪肉、香菇、虾仁和莲子做额外的馅料。后者的制作过程要简单得多。把苏打水放在捆扎好的大米里,蒸透后味道更软更滑。

嘉兴风味

嘉兴粽子在端午节期间很受欢迎。最常见的馅料有豆沙、鲜肉、莲子、龙眼和花生,呈三角金字塔状。不同的是,一些肥肉会混合在馅料中,这样在煮了几个小时后,用猪肉煮出来的油看起来会呈亮黄色,尝起来有脂肪,但不油腻。

北京风味

作为北方城市的代表,北京粽子比南方地区的粽子小,通常呈金字塔形,馅料通常是豆子、枣子和莲子。肉很少用作馅料,所以大多数粽子都有甜味。

上海风味

上海粽子风味浓郁,配料丰富,有鲜肉、香菇、板栗、蛋黄、烤鸭、红豆等。功德林餐厅售卖的素食粽子很不错,有蘑菇粽、豆沙粽、松子米粽等。此外,沈大成还发明了最独特的风味粽,如咖喱鸡粽子。

台湾风味

台湾粽子的味道和福建粽子相似。最受欢迎的两种风格是成家肉宗和八味粽。当地人习惯用各种肉和海鲜做粽子,所以大多数都有咸和甜的味道。

参考答案

Exercises

Ⅰ. 1—6 f a b c e d

Ⅱ. 1. lunar month

2. maximun

3. the Tomb-Sweeping Day and the Mid-Autumn Festival

4. dragon boat racing; eating Zongzi

5. sticky rice ball

Ⅲ. 1. 端午节就快到了。

2. 如果我们能休息几天就好了。

3. 今年端午节 6 月 7 日开始,我们 10 日回学校上学。

4. 人们大多认为端午节的由来跟屈原紧密相关。

5. He was a patriotic poet who wrote a lot of works to show his care and devotion to his country.

6. In his sorrow Qu Yuan threw himself into the Miluo River.

7. That is really a story ends in tragedy.

8. Once I went more deep into his whole life story, I felt extremely sad and sorry for him.

Ⅳ. Omitted

Lesson 3   The Lantern Festival   元宵节

Warm-Up

Work in pairs. Learn the following words and phrases. Then answer the following questions.

1. When is the Lantern Festival?
2. Do you set off fireworks on the Lantern Festival?

Words and Expressions

Read the following words and expressions. Then try to memorize them.

festival *n.* 节日	in my opinion 在我看来，依我之见
lantern riddles 灯谜	lion dance 舞狮
dragon dance 舞龙	yangge dance 扭秧歌
land boat dance 划旱船	walking on stilts 踩高跷
rice dumplings 元宵	glutinous rice flour 糯米粉
coconut *n.* 椰子	sesame *n.* 芝麻

Useful Expressions

1. Which festival in China do you think is the most gorgeous?
2. Is it even grander than the Spring Festival?
3. It is more colorful than the first day of the Spring Festival.
4. Is there any interesting tradition during the Lantern Festival?
5. Guessing lantern riddles is an important part of the festival.
6. What special food do people eat on that day? Jiaozi?

Dialogue

Watch the animation, then practice the dialogue by reading it aloud with your partner. Read it through at least twice, and change your role each time.

(**Scene:** Sally is a college student in Cultural and Tourism School from China. Sam is an exchange student from America. In the classroom at campus, Sally is talking with Sam, who is very curious about Chinese festivals.)

Sally: Sam, which festival in China do you think is the most gorgeous?

Sam: Maybe the Spring Festival, am I right?

Sally: Well, in my opinion, the Lantern Festival is the most gorgeous.

Sam: Why? Is it even grander than the Spring Festival?

Sally: Yes, it is the last day of the Spring Festival, symbolizing the coming of spring. It is more colorful than the first day of the Spring Festival.

Sam: Colorful? Is there any interesting tradition during the Lantern Festival?

Sally: Yes, of course. There are both fireworks and lantern displays on that day. They can be found almost everywhere, especially in the square of town center and at temples.

Sam: People just watch fireworks and observe the lanterns?

Sally: Of course not. Guessing lantern riddles is an important part of the festival.

Sam: Anything else?

Sally: There are performances such as the lion dance, the dragon dance, the yangge dance, the land boat dance, walking on stilts, and so on.

Sam: What special food do people eat on that day? Jiaozi?

Sally: No, we eat Yuanxiao, that is rice dumplings.

Sam: What are Yuanxiao?

Sally: They are small balls made of glutinous rice flour with sesame or peanuts or walnut meat as filling.

Questions:

1. Is there any interesting tradition during the Lantern Festival?
2. What special food do people eat on the Lantern Festival?
3. What are Yuanxiao?
4. Is the Lantern Festival the most gorgeous festival in China? Why?

Role-Play

Act it out according to the instructions.

A student from China: Sally

1. To greet Sam and extend welcome to him.

Lesson 3   The Lantern Festival   元宵节

2. Sally tells Sam something about the Lantern Festival, and explains its customs.
3. Sally tells Sam the special food of the Lantern Festival.

A student from America: Sam
1. To greet Sally.
2. To show curiosity about the Chinese Festivals.
3. To ask the special food of the Lantern Festival.

📑 Passage Reading

The Lantern Festival, also known as the Shang Yuan Festival, is the last day of the Spring Festival, and one of the most important traditional festivals of China. According to legends, it was after the Han and Wei Dynasties that the Lantern Festival became a folk festival. Since Tang Dynasty, lighting lanterns has become a folk custom.

On the Lantern Festival, there are a series of traditional folk activities such as watching lanterns, guessing riddles, setting off fireworks, and eating Yuanxiao, or you may call it Tangyuan, symbolizing "family reunion", since the words "Tangyuan" and "Reunion" are similar in pronunciation.

In addition, the lion dance, the dragon dance, the yangge dance, the land boat dance, walking on stilts… have also become the traditional folk performances on the festival. In June 2008, the Lantern Festival was included in the list of national intangible cultural heritage. Its cultural and social values have extraordinary significance.

Useful Words and Expressions:

watching lanterns 赏花灯	guessing riddles 猜灯谜
setting off fireworks 放烟花	family reunion 家庭团圆
traditional *a.* 传统的	folk *a.* 民间的
performances *n.* 表演	intangible cultural heritage 非物质文化遗产

Translation Tasks:
1. 元宵节也称为上元节，是春节的最后一天。
2. 相传在汉魏之后元宵节才成为民间节日。
3. 自唐代以来，点灯笼已成为民俗。
4. 2008 年 6 月，元宵节被列入国家非物质文化遗产名录。

5. On the Lantern Festival, there are a series of traditional folk activities such as watching lanterns, guessing riddles, setting off fireworks, and eating Yuanxiao.

Exercises

I. Match the following words and phrases, and write the corresponding letter for each item.

1. watching lanterns　　_____　　a. 表演
2. guessing riddles　　_____　　b. 元宵
3. setting off fireworks　　_____　　c. 放烟花
4. traditional　　_____　　d. 糯米粉
5. folk　　_____　　e. 椰子
6. performances　　_____　　f. 芝麻
7. rice dumplings　　_____　　g. 赏花灯
8. glutinous rice flour　　_____　　h. 猜灯谜
9. coconut　　_____　　i. 传统的
10. sesame　　_____　　j. 民间的

II. Fill in the blanks according to the text.

1. Which _____ in China do you think is the most gorgeous?
2. _____ is the most gorgeous.
3. The Lantern Festival is the _____ of Chinese Spring Festival, symbolizing the coming of the spring.
4. Is there any interesting _____ during the Lantern Festival?
5. _____ is an important part of the festival.

III. Translate the following sentences according to the dialogue.

1. Well, in my opinion, the Lantern Festival is the most gorgeous.
2. Is it even grander than the Spring Festival?
3. It is more colorful than the first day of the Spring Festival.
4. There are both fireworks and lantern displays on that day.
5. People just watch fireworks and observe the lanterns?

IV. Work in pairs and discuss the following questions.

1. How do you think of the Lantern Festival?
2. Do you like Yuanxiao? Why?

Lesson 3　The Lantern Festival　元宵节

➡️ Knowledge Expansion

The Lantern Festival falls on the 15th day of the first lunar month, the night of the first full moon following the Spring Festival. The origins of the Lantern Festival are related to ancient humanity's use of fire to celebrate festivals and avert disaster. Since the Lantern Festival involves making offerings to the deities and is celebrated at night, it is natural that fire would play an important role. Over time, the Lantern Festival gradually evolved into its present form.

Eating Yuanxiao is one of the special traditions of the Lantern Festival. There are many different types of Yuanxiao, with fillings covering the entire range of the five flavors (savory, spicy, sweet, sour, and salty). Sweet fillings are the most common, and include sweet bean paste, sesame, peanut, etc. Eating Yuanxiao at home is only one part of the Lantern Festival. Even more important is the tradition of attending temple fairs or street fairs and viewing lantern displays.

Many Chinese holidays involve lanterns. But the Lantern Festival represents the epitome of this custom. Lanterns are first brought out on the thirteenth day of the first lunar month. They are tested on the fourteenth, formally lit on the fifteenth, and taken down on the eighteenth. The Lantern Festival not only provids a beautiful show of multicolored lanterns, but also featurs a wide range of folk art and performances, such as the lion dance, the dragon dance, the Yangge dance, the land boat dance, and walking on stilts.

(Excerpted from www.bing.com)

参考译文

课文阅读

元宵节，又称上元节，是春节的最后一天，是中国最重要的传统节日之一。

相传在汉魏之后，元宵节才成为民间节日。自唐代以来，点灯笼已成为民俗。

元宵节有一系列传统的民俗活动，例如赏花灯、猜谜语、放烟花、吃元宵，元宵也可以称为汤圆，象征"团圆"，因为"汤圆"这个词和"团圆"的发音相似。

此外，舞狮、舞龙、秧歌、划旱船、踩高跷等也成为节日的传统民间表演。2008年6月，元宵节被列入国家非物质文化遗产名录。它的文化和社会价值具有非凡的意义。

扩展阅读

元宵节是农历正月十五，即春节后的第一个满月之夜。元宵节的起源与古代人类使用火庆祝节日和避灾有关。由于在元宵节要向神灵供奉，并且是在夜晚庆祝，因此灯笼自然而然地起着重要作用。随着时间的流逝，元宵节逐渐演变成现在的形式。

吃元宵是元宵节的特殊传统之一，元宵种类繁多，馅料包括五种风味（咸、辣、甜、酸、咸）。甜馅是最常见的，包括豆沙、芝麻、花生等。在家吃元宵只是元宵节的一部分。更重要的传统是参加庙会或街头集市和赏花灯。

许多中国的节日涉及灯笼。但是元宵节是这一习俗的缩影。灯笼是在农历正月十三拿出来，十四进行测试，在十五正式点亮，并在十八拆除。元宵节不仅有五彩灯笼的精彩表演，而且还有多种民间艺术和表演，例如舞狮、舞龙、秧歌、划旱船、踩高跷等。

参考答案

Exercises

Ⅰ. 1—5　g h c i j　　6—10　a b d e f

Ⅱ. 1. festival
2. The Lantern Festival
3. last day
4. tradition
5. Guessing Lantern riddles

Ⅲ. 1. 我认为元宵节是最华丽的。
2. 它比春节还要盛大吗？
3. 它比春节的第一天更加丰富多彩。
4. 那天有烟火和花灯展览。
5. 人们只是看烟花、赏花灯吗？

Ⅳ. Omitted

Lesson 4 The Mid-Autumn Festival 中秋节

Warm-Up

Work in pairs. Learn the following words and phrases. Then answer the following questions.

1. When is the Mid-Autumn Festival?
2. There are many traditional customs on the Mid-Autumn Festival, what are they?

Words and Expressions

Read the following words and expressions. Then try to memorize them.

celebrate *v.* 庆祝	family reunion 家庭团聚
the Mid-Autumn Festival 中秋节	would rather *n.* 宁愿
in that case 在那种情况下	prefer *v.* 更喜欢
expire *v.* 过期	variety *n.* 多样,多样性,变化
varieties of 各种各样的	

Useful Expressions

1. We will have a family reunion, eating moon cakes and watching the full moon at night.
2. That's because they are finely wrapped and the wrapping is even more valuable than the cakes.
3. I would rather wait after the Mid-Autumn Festival. They would be much cheaper.
4. Most of the cakes will become expired before we can eat them and will be thrown away.
5. There are hundreds of varieties of moon cakes, which flavors do you like?
6. I like all kinds of flavors!

Dialogue

Watch the animation, then practice the dialogue by reading it aloud with your partner. Read it through at least twice, and change your role each time.

(**Scene:** Sally is a college student in Cultural and Tourism School from China. Sam is an exchange student from America. In the classroom at campus, Sally is talking with Sam, who is very curious about Chinese festivals.)

Sam: Sally, the Mid-Autumn Festival is coming soon, how will you celebrate it?

Sally: We will have a family reunion, eating the moon cakes and watching the full moon at night.

Sam: Oh, the moon cakes! I like the moon cakes! But the moon cakes are so expensive!

Sally: Yes, that's true. That's because they are finely wrapped and the wrapping is even more valuable than the cakes.

Sam: I would rather wait after the Mid-Autumn Festival. They would be much cheaper.

Sally: Good idea! But I have a better idea, that is, I can give you some, since my father can always receive a lot of moon cakes from friends and relatives. Most of the cakes will become expired before we can eat them and will be thrown away.

Sam: Oh, if you can't finish eating them this year, give them to me, I can eat them all.

Sally: No problem, but there are hundreds of varieties of the moon cakes, which flavors do you like? For example, mixed nuts, mashed beans, lotus-seed paste, egg yolk paste, pork floss, and so on.

Sam: I like all kinds of flavors!

Sally: How about joining us? Would you like to come to my home on the Mid-Autumn Festival?

Sam: Yes, I'd love to!

Questions:

1. How will Sally celebrate the coming Mid-Autumn Festival?
2. What special food do people eat on the Mid-Autumn Festival?
3. There are hundreds of varieties of the moon cakes, which flavors does Sam like?
4. Will Sam come to Sally's home on the Mid-Autumn Festival?

Role-Play

Act it out according to the instructions.

A student from China: Sally

1. To greet Sam and extend welcome to him.
2. Sally tells Sam something about the Mid-Autumn Festival, and explains its customs.
3. Sally tells Sam the special food of the Mid-Autumn Festival.

Lesson 4　The Mid-Autumn Festival　中秋节

A student from America: Sam
1. To greet Sally.
2. To show curiosity about the Chinese festivals.
3. To ask the special food of the Mid-Autumn Festival.

Passage Reading

The Mid-Autumn Festival is on the 15th day of August according to the lunar calendar; it is a Chinese festival that is held to celebrate the end of the summer harvest, when the crops have been gathered. The Mid-Autumn Festival began in the early years of the Tang Dynasty, prevailing in the Song Dynasty, and by the Ming and Qing Dynasties, it has become one of the major Chinese festivals, being considered as important as the Spring Festival. Influenced by Chinese culture, the Mid-Autumn Festival is also a traditional festival for some Chinese living abroad, especially for those living in East Asia and Southeast Asia.

Since 2008, the Mid-Autumn Festival has been listed as an official national holiday. In 2006, the Mid-Autumn Festival was included in the first batch of national intangible cultural heritage by the State Council. There are many traditional customs on the Mid-Autumn Festival, such as, worshipping the moon, watching the moon, eating moon cakes, etc., which have been passed down to the present. On the Mid-Autumn Festival night, people look up to the sky, seeing the full moon and naturally expecting family reunion. People who live or work far away from their homes will try to come back for the family reunion. Therefore, the Mid-Autumn Festival is also known as the "Reunion Festival". On that day people not only celebrate the family reunion, but also pray for a good harvest and happiness, thus making it a colorful and precious cultural heritage. The Mid-Autumn Festival, the Dragon Boat Festival, the Spring Festival, and the Tomb-Sweeping Day are also known as the four traditional festivals in China.

On the Mid-Autumn Festival, people have the custom of eating the moon cakes to show "family reunion". The moon cakes are also known as the reunion cakes. According to legend, in ancient China, the emperor had rituals of worshipping the sun in spring and the moon in autumn. At that time, the moon cakes were the offerings to worship the moon god. Later, people gradually take the moon cake as a symbol of family reunion. Now the moon cakes have become the must-have gifts for family or friends during the Mid-Autumn Festival. The moon cake fillings mainly include fruits, plants and plant seeds, such as cranberry, lotus root, walnuts, almonds, sesame seeds, melon seeds, lotus seeds, red beans… and even include ham, egg yolk, pork floss and abalone.

Useful Words and Expressions:

lunar calendar 阴历	the State Council 国务院
cranberry n. 蔓越莓	walnut n. 核桃
almond n. 杏仁	sesame n. 芝麻
melon seeds 瓜子	lotus seeds 莲子
egg yolk 蛋黄	pork floss 肉松
abalone n. 鲍鱼	blood vessels 血管
immunity n. 免疫力	

Translation Tasks:

1. 中秋节是农历八月十五日。
2. 自2008年以来，中秋节被列为国家法定节假日。
3. 中秋节有许多传承至今的传统习俗，如祭月、赏月、吃月饼等。
4. 在中秋节的夜晚，人们仰望天空，看到满月，自然期待家庭团聚。
5. The Mid-Autumn Festival is also known as the "Reunion Festival".
6. On the Mid-Autumn Festival, people have the custom of eating the moon cakes to show "family reunion".
7. The moon cakes are also known as the reunion cakes.
8. Now the moon cakes have become the must-have gifts for family or friends during the Mid-Autumn Festivals.

➡ Exercises

I. Match the following words and phrases, and write the corresponding letter for each item.

1. melon seeds _____   a. 蔓越莓
2. lotus seeds _____   b. 核桃
3. egg yolk _____   c. 杏仁
4. abalone _____   d. 芝麻
5. blood vessels _____   e. 瓜子
6. immunity _____   f. 莲子
7. cranberry _____   g. 蛋黄

8. walnut　　　　_____　　　h. 鲍鱼
9. almond　　　　_____　　　i. 血管
10. sesame　　　　_____　　　j. 免疫力

II. Fill in the blanks according to the text.

1. The Mid-Autumn Festival is on the 15th day of August according to _____.

2. The Mid-Autumn Festival is also a _____ festival for some Chinese living abroad.

3. Since 2008, the Mid-Autumn Festival has been listed as a _____ .

4. On the Mid-Autumn Festival, people have the custom of eating _____ to show "family reunion".

5. The moon cake _____ mainly include fruits, plants and plant seeds.

III. Translate the following sentences according to the dialogue.

1. The Mid-Autumn Festival is coming soon, how will you celebrate it?

2. I like the moon cakes! But the moon cakes are so expensive!

3. I would rather wait after the Mid-Autumn Day. They would be much cheaper.

4. Most of the cakes will become expired before we can eat them and will be thrown away.

5. Would you like to come to my home on the Mid-Autumn Festival?

IV. Work in pairs and discuss the following questions.

1. How do you think of the Mid-Autumn Festival?

2. Do you like the moon cakes? Why?

▶ Knowledge Expansion

Held on the 15th day of the 8th lunar month, the Mid-Autumn Festival is the second grandest festival after the Spring Festival in China. The Mid-Autumn Festival is an evening celebration when families gather together to light lanterns, eat moon cakes and appreciate the round moon. On that night, the moon appears to be at its roundest and brightest. The full moon is a symbol for family reunion, which is why that day is also known as the festival of reunion.

This festival is celebrated by the Chinese and the people of some southeastern Asian countries. Although it is celebrated on the same day, each country has different customs on the celebration. Most workers can have one day off during the day.

The Mid-Autumn Festival celebrations date back to more than 2,000 years ago. In those times, the Chinese emperors prayed to Heaven for a prosperous year. In Mid-Autumn, the farmers have just finished gathering their crops and bringing in fruits from the orchards. They are overwhelmed with joy when they have a bumper harvest and at the same time, they feel quite relaxed after a year of hard work. So the 15th day of the eighth lunar month has gradually evolved as a widely celebrated festival for ordinary people.

(Excerpted from www.bing.com)

参考译文

课文阅读

中秋节是农历八月十五日。这是在庄稼收割完毕之后为了庆祝夏季收获庄稼结束的一个中国节日。中秋节开始于唐朝初期，盛行于宋代，明清时期它已成为中国的主要节日之一，被认为是和春节同样重要的节日。受中国文化的影响，中秋节对于一些在国外生活的中国人来说也是一个传统的节日，特别是对于那些生活在东亚和东南亚地区的人们。

自2008年以来，中秋节被列为国家法定节假日。2006年，中秋节被国务院列入首批国家级非物质文化遗产名录。中秋节有许多传承至今的传统习俗，如祭月、赏月、吃月饼等。在中秋节的夜晚，人们仰望天空，看到满月，自然期待家庭团聚。远离家乡生活或工作的人们会尽量回来与家人团聚。因此，中秋节也被称为"团圆节"。当天人们不仅庆祝家庭团聚，还祈求丰收和幸福，使其成为丰富多彩的珍贵文化遗产。中秋节、端午节、春节和清明节也被称为中国四大传统节日。

在中秋节，人们习惯用吃月饼来表示"家庭团圆"。月饼又称团圆饼。据传说，在中国古代，皇帝有春天祭日、秋天祭月的仪式。当时，月饼是祭祀月神的祭品。后来，人们逐渐将吃月饼作为家庭团聚的象征。现在月饼已经成为中秋节期间送给家人或朋友的必备礼品。月饼馅料主要包括水果、植物和植物种子，如蔓越莓、莲藕、核桃、杏仁、芝麻、瓜子、莲子、红豆……甚至包括火腿、蛋黄、肉松和鲍鱼。

扩展阅读

中秋节在农历八月十五日，是仅次于春节的第二大节日。中秋节就是一场晚会，家庭成员聚集在一起点亮灯笼、吃月饼、欣赏圆月。在那天晚上，月亮似乎是最圆和最亮的。满月是家庭团聚的象征，这就是这一天也被称为团圆节的原因。

这个节日是由中国人以及一些东南亚国家的人民庆祝的。尽管庆祝活动是在同一天举行的，但每个国家的庆祝活动都有不同的习俗。大多数情况下，员工白天可以休息一天。

中秋节的庆祝活动可以追溯到2,000多年前。当时是皇帝向上苍祈祷繁荣年。中秋时节，农民刚刚收割完农作物，并从果园里收获了水果。当他们获得丰收时会感到非常高兴，与此同时，经过一年的努力他们感到非常放松。因此，农历八月十五日已逐渐演变为一个普天同庆节日。

Lesson 4　The Mid-Autumn Festival　中秋节

参考答案

Exercises

Ⅰ. 1—5　e f g h i　6—10　j a b c d

Ⅱ. 1. the lunar calender

　　2. traditional

　　3. national legal holiday

　　4. the moon cakes

　　5. fillings

Ⅲ. 1. 中秋节快到了，你将如何庆祝呢？

　　2. 我喜欢月饼！但是月饼太贵了！

　　3. 我宁愿等到在中秋节之后。它们会便宜得多。

　　4. 大多数月饼在我们吃之前就过期了，它们将会被扔掉。

　　5. 你想在中秋节来我家吗？

Ⅳ. Omitted

Unit VIII
Chinese Customs

风土人情

Lesson 1　Chinese Paper-Cuts　剪纸

Warm-Up

Work in pairs. Learn the following words and phrases. Then answer the following questions.

1. Can you make some simple paper cutting? And what are these steps?
2. Do you know the culture of Chinese paper cutting?

Words and Expressions

Read the following words and expressions. Then try to memorize them.

enduring *a.* 持久的	enshrine *v.* 珍藏；铭记
upcoming *a.* 即将到来的	WeChat *n.* 微信
flyer *n.* 传单	proceed *v.* 继续进行；接着做
QR code 二维码	

Useful Expressions

1. I'm planning to go to Beijing this weekend to explore Chinese paper-cut.
2. Is the course friendly for entry level learners like me?
3. The price is 330 yuan per person, including finger food, all materials, and a wooden frame for your paper cutting.
4. During the workshop you'll learn the basics of paper-cut.
5. Chinese paper-cut is a traditional folk craft.

Dialogue

Watch the animation, then practice the dialogue by reading it aloud with your partner. Read it through at least twice, and change your role each time.

(**Scene:** Sally is a college student in Cultural and Tourism School from China. Sam is an exchange student from America. Sam wants to learn paper cutting, so Sally tells him where to

Lesson 1　Chinese Paper-Cuts　剪纸

study this traditional art.)

Sally: Hey, Sam, what's happening?

Sam: Not much, sally, but I'm planning to go to Beijing this weekend to explore Chinese paper-cut.

Sally: Yeah, sounds good. Chinese paper-cut is a traditional folk craft. With its long history and enduring popularity, it is known as a treasure in Chinese folk arts and becomes one enshrinement in world treasure house.

Sam: So, where do you suggest visiting?

Sally: The upcoming workshop "paper, scissors" scheduled for short term, is a good place to learn and explore paper-cut. Would you like to join?

Sam: Great idea! Any details about the workshop?

Sally: Yeah, during the workshop you'll learn the basics of paper-cut.

Sam: Is the course friendly for entry level learners like me?

Sally: Sure. They follow the step-by-step teaching method, and they will encourage you to fulfill your tasks.

Sam: How about the price?

Sally: Well, let me check it out, err… The price is 330 yuan per person, including finger food, all materials, and a wooden frame for your paper cutting.

Sam: That's pretty nice.

Sally: You can pre-pay on WeChat. When you get the chance to view their event flyer on your computer, just scan the QR code and proceed with the payment.

Questions:

1. What is Sam going to do on weekend?
2. Is there a suitable course for the beginners to learn paper cutting?

➡ Role-Play

Act it out according to the instructions.

A student from China: Sally

1. Greetings.
2. Sally recommends that he take part in a course for paper cutting.

A student from America: Sam

1. Greetings.
2. Sam wants to learn some Chinese traditional crafts.
3. Sam gets some suggestions from Sally.

Passage Reading

Paper cutting is a unique form of folk art in China, with a history of more than two thousand years. It is very likely that paper cutting stemmed from Han Dynasty, which followed the invention of paper. Since then, it was popularized in plenty of places in China. The materials and tools which can be used for paper cutting are rather simple: paper and a scissor. The paper cutting works are usually made of red paper, because the red color is related to "the happiness" in the Chinese traditional culture. Therefore, the red paper cutting works are the first choice for the decoration of windows and doors in pleasant occasions such as wedding ceremony and the Spring Festival.

Useful Words and Expressions:

stem from 起源于

plenty of 大量

popularize v. 普及；使通俗化

wedding ceremony 婚礼

Translation Tasks:

1. 剪纸很可能源于汉代。
2. 剪纸在中国的许多地方得到了普及。
3. 因为红色在中国传统文化中与幸福相联系。
4. Paper cutting is a unique form of folk art in China.
5. The red paper cutting works are the first choice for the decoration of windows and doors in pleasant occasions.

Exercises

I. *Match the following words and phrases, and write the corresponding letter for each item.*

1. enshrinement   _____   a. 二维码
2. material   _____   b. 民间艺术
3. occasion   _____   c. 珍藏
4. QR code   _____   d. 材料

Lesson 1　Chinese Paper-Cuts　剪纸

5. stem from　　　　_____　　e. 传单
6. popularize　　　　_____　　f. 根源是
7. enduring　　　　 _____　　g. 持久的
8. flyer　　　　　　_____　　h. 仪式
9. fork arts　　　　 _____　　i. 场合
10. ceremony　　　　_____　　j. 普及

Ⅱ. *Fill in the blanks according to the text.*

1. We just need _____ to make some paper cutting.
2. In Chinese traditional culture, red color represents _____.
3. The fee of the course for beginners includes _____.
4. Paper cutting originated from _____.
5. Paper cutting is considered as _____ in the Chinese folk arts.

Ⅲ. *Translate the following sentences according to the dialogue.*

1. With its long history and enduring popularity, it is known as a treasure in Chinese folk arts and becomes one enshrinement in world treasure house.
2. The price is 330 yuan per person, including finger food, all materials, and a wooden frame for your paper cutting.
3. Is the course friendly for entry level learners like me?
4. When you get the chance to view their event flyer on your computer, just scan the QR code and proceed with the payment.
5. They follow the step-by-step teaching method, and they will encourage you to fulfill your tasks.

Ⅳ. *Work in pairs and discuss the following questions.*

1. What are the benefits that Chinese paper cutting brings us?
2. Why do we hand down paper-cut art from generation to generation?

Knowledge Expansion

　　China has a history of more than five thousand years. As a result, there are many traditional arts that have been inherited, such as paper cutting. It is a kind of amazing art. People can use scissors to cut different shapes, like flowers and animals. When foreigners see the paper cutting, they are surprised and give big applause to this great art.

　　People find hope and comfort in expressing wishes with paper cuttings. For example: for a wedding ceremony, the red paper cuttings are a traditional and required decoration on the tea set, the dressing table glass, and other furniture. A big red paper character "Xi" (happiness) is a traditional must on the newly-wed's door. Upon the birthday party of a senior, the character "Shou" represents longevity and will add delight to the whole celebration; while a pattern of plump children cuddling fish signifies that every year, they will be abundant in wealth.

At wedding ceremony, paper-cut "Fish playing around lotus" "Fish biting lotus" "Lotus bearing seeds" and "Happy dolls" (baby with coiled hair holding a pair of fish) are pasted on the ceiling of the bridal chamber.

Fish, being a proliferous legendary animal, is often used to symbolize having multiple children. A yin-yang paired fish has become a cultural code in the Chinese folk-art works.

Today, when technology takes control of most fields, some traditional arts have lost their markets and the young people start to forget about these treasures. We need to learn more about these traditional arts, so as to better preserve them. Schools can open courses to let students learn these arts.

参考译文

课文阅读

剪纸是中国一种独特的传统民间艺术形式，已有两千多年的历史。剪纸起源于汉朝，它伴随着纸张的发明而出现。从那时起，剪纸在中国许多地方得到了普及。剪纸的材料和工具很简单：纸和剪刀。剪纸作品通常是用红纸做的，因为在中国传统文化中，红色与"幸福"有关。因此，红色剪纸作品是婚礼、春节等喜庆场合门窗装饰的首选。

扩展阅读

中国有着五千多年的历史，因此，有许多传统艺术被传承下来，如剪纸。这是一种神奇的艺术，人们可以用剪刀剪出许多不一样的形状，如花、动物。当外国人看到剪纸时，他们非常的惊讶，并对这一伟大的艺术给予了热烈的掌声。

人们通过剪纸表达愿望，寻求希望和慰藉。例如，在婚礼仪式上，红色的剪纸作为一种传统的、必要的装饰，出现在茶具、梳妆台镜以及其他家具上。一个大红的"囍"字（幸福）作为一种传统，必须贴在婚礼会场的大门上。在长者的寿宴上，"寿"字代表长寿，将为整个庆祝活动增加喜悦；而胖乎乎的孩子拥抱鱼的图案表示他们每年都会收获丰富的财富。

在婚礼仪式上，剪纸"鱼戏莲花""鱼咬莲花""莲花结子"，以及"快乐娃娃"（有着卷曲头发的宝宝抱着一对鱼）被粘贴在"洞房"的天花板上。

鱼是传说中多子的神兽，寓意多子多孙。配对的阴阳鱼成为中国民间艺术作品的文化

Lesson 1　Chinese Paper-Cuts　剪纸

代码。

　　今天，技术占据了大部分领域，一些传统艺术已经失去了市场，年轻人开始忘记这些宝藏。我们需要更多地了解这些传统艺术，为了更好地保护它们，学校可以开设课程让学生学习相关艺术。

参考答案

Exercises

Ⅰ. 1—5　c d i a f　　6—10　j g e b h

Ⅱ. 1. paper and a scissor

2. happiness

3. finger food, all materials, and a wooden frame for your paper cutting

4. Han Dynasty

5. a treasure

Ⅲ. 1. 中国剪纸是传统的民间工艺。它有着悠久的历史和经久不衰的名气，被誉为中国民间艺术的瑰宝，是世界宝库中的珍品。

2. 价格是每人330元，包括小吃、全部材料和一个木框，可以用来剪纸。

3. 这个课程适合像我这样的初学者吗？

4. 当你有机会在你的计算机上看到他们的活动传单时，只需扫描二维码并付款。

5. 他们会采用循序渐进的教学方法，鼓励你完成你的任务。

Ⅳ. Omitted

Lesson 2 Chinese Kites 风筝

Warm-Up

Work in pairs. Learn the following words and phrases. Then answer the following questions.

1. What sports do you usually do?
2. Have you ever flown a kite before? How did you feel about it?

Words and Expressions

Read the following words and expressions. Then try to memorize them.

The Tomb-Sweeping Day 清明节	commemorate *v.* 纪念；作为……的纪念
invent *v.* 发明；创造	philosopher *n.* 哲学家；哲人
the Warring States Period 战国时期	amusements *n.* 娱乐
since *conj.* 由于；因为；既然	

Useful Expressions

1. I do know a little about it.
2. It was made of wood and was used to pass messages.
3. These days people fly kites for fun and as a type of sport for better health.
4. It was invented by the philosopher Mozi in the Warring States period.
5. Shall we fly a kite this afternoon since there is no class?

Dialogue

Watch the animation, then practice the dialogue by reading it aloud with your partner. Read it through at least twice, and change your role each time.

(**Scene:** Sally is a college student in Cultural and Tourism School from China. Sam is an exchange student from America. At campus, Sally and Sam are talking about what they did during the Tomb-sweeping Day, and Sally shares some knowledge about the kite with Sam.)

Sam: Hi, Sally. What did you do for the Tomb-Sweeping Day?
Sally: I went with my parents to sweep the tombs to commemorate our ancestors. How about you?

Lesson 2 Chinese Kites 风筝

Sam: Oh. I flew a kite with my friends. It was fun. By the way, you know about kite, right?

Sally: Yes. I do know a little about it. It was invented by the philosopher Mozi in the Warring States period. It was made of wood and was used to pass messages.

Sam: So, it was first invented for communications instead of amusements during the war time. I didn't know that before.

Sally: These days people fly kites for fun and as a type of sport for better health.

Sam: Shall we fly a kite this afternoon since there is no class?

Sally: Why not? Let's do it.

Questions:

1. Who first invented the kite?
2. What was the kite made of in the Warring State Period?
3. During the war time, what was the kite used for?
4. What is the Tomb-Sweeping Day?

Role-Play

Act it out according to the instructions.

A student from China: Sally

1. To greet Sam.
2. Sally tells him she flies a kite with her parents.
3. Sally tells him the ways of flying a kite and making a kite.

A student from America: Sam

1. To greet Sally.
2. To ask what Sally did during holidays.
3. To ask how to fly a kite and how to make a kite.

Passage Reading

The tradition of flying a kite is attributed to the Warring States Period. It is said that Mozi, a philosopher of the early Warring States Period, spent three years in making a wooden bird, which is the original form of kite.

Later, Lu Ban, a legendary carpenter, improved the kite by using bamboo. By the Western Han Dynasty, Han Xin, an expert on military affairs, further improved the kite with paper to make surveys for military purposes.

Now kite flying is not only for the common people, but also for the competition of the kite experts. The international kite festival is held annually on April 20 to 25 in Weifang, Shandong Province, which attracts a large number of Chinese and foreigners.

Useful Words and Expressions:

attribute to 归因于；认为……是由于	original *a.* 起初的；最早的
survey *n.* 调查；勘测	legendary *a.* 传奇的；传说的
dynasty *n.* 朝代；王朝	military affairs 军事；军务
expert *n.* 专家；行家	annually *ad.* 每年；一年一次

Translation Tasks:

1. The tradition of flying a kite is attributed to the Warring States Period.
2. It is said that Mozi, a philosopher of the early Warring States Period, spent three years in making a wooden bird, which is the original form of kite.
3. Later, Lu Ban, a legendary carpenter, improved the kite by using bamboo.
4. Now kite flying is not only for the common people, but also for the competition of the kite experts.
5. The international kite festival is held annually on April 20 to 25 in Weifang, Shandong Province, which attracts a large number of Chinese and foreigners.

Exercises

I. *Match the following words and phrases, and write the corresponding letter for each item.*

1. carpenter　　　　_____　　a. 比赛
2. form　　　　　　_____　　b. 祖先
3. military purpose　_____　　c. 军事用途
4. communication　_____　　d. 木匠
5. amusement　　　_____　　e. 战国时期
6. province　　　　_____　　f. 形状
7. ancestor　　　　_____　　g. 朝代
8. the Warring States Period　_____　　h. 通信
9. competition　　_____　　i. 娱乐
10. dynasty　　　　_____　　j. 省份

II. *Fill in the blanks according to the text.*

1. The tradition of flying a kite originated from _____.

2. The first kite was made of _____.
3. The international kite festival is held in _____ every year.
4. _____ improved the kite by using bamboo.
5. By the Western Han Dynasty, the kite was used for _____.

III. *Translate the following sentences according to the dialogue.*

1. I went with my parents to sweep the tombs to commemorate our ancestors.
2. It was first invented for communications instead of amusements during the war time.
3. These days people fly kites for fun and as a type of sport for better health.
4. It was invented by the philosopher Mozi in the Warring States period.
5. It was made of wood and was used to pass messages.

IV. *Work in pairs and discuss the following questions.*

1. Can you briefly introduce different kinds of kite?
2. Have you made a kite before? Please share your method of making a kite with your partner.

Knowledge Expansion

Kites usually represent mythological characters, symbolic creatures, as well as legendary figures. Some have whistles or strings designed to make unique sounds while flying. We can divide them into two categories: large and small kites. Today, you will see people flying small kites with children in many Chinese parks. You can also see adults flying the larger kites and using more advanced methods with larger ropes to support the great size.

Ancient Kite Construction

Kite construction consists of three parts: framing, gluing and decoration. With framing, light woods such as bamboo were often used to create the bones of the kite. These are both light, exceptionally strong, and pliable. Many frame shapes were popular, including traditional representations of birds, butterflies and dragonflies, as well as non-winged insects such as centipedes or mythical animals like dragons.

Modern Kite Construction

Modern kite artisans go beyond the tradition, producing kites that conform to the creator's imagination. Materials such as plastic and nylon allow for bright colors and enhanced durability. LED lights and specialized noise makers also enhance the kite flying and viewing experience. Sometimes movement is incorporated into a kite by means of a hinged arrangement of sections of the frame, suggesting wing or tail movement, etc.

The Weifang Kite Tradition

The city of Weifang, Shandong Province, has a special relationship to the kite. The city is the home to the International Kite Association, and holds the Weifang International Kite Festival from April 20th to the 25th each year. Kite enthusiasts in the thousands, and from all corners of the globe, descend upon the city of Weifang at this time each year to participate in the kite competitions. Tourists flock just to watch this majestic and colorful spectacle. The climax of the festival is the crowning of the annual "Kite King". Weifang also has a museum dedicated to the history of the kite.

In the History of Flight pavilion at the National Aeronautics and Space Museum in Washington D.C. a plaque is inscribed to the Chinese kite. It states, "The earliest aircraft made by man were the kites and missiles of ancient China."

参考译文

课文阅读

风筝的传统要从战国时期说起。据说，在战国时期，哲学家墨子花了三年的时间制作了一只木鸟，这就是最早的风筝。

后来，传奇的木匠鲁班用竹子改良了风筝。到了西汉时期，军事家韩信又进一步把风筝做了改良，用纸来制作，用于军事的调查。

现在，不仅普通人可以放风筝，风筝爱好者还会进行风筝比赛。国际风筝节于每年4月20日—25日在山东潍坊举办，吸引了大量的中外友人。

扩展阅读

风筝通常代表神话人物、生物以及传奇人物。有些风筝有哨子或琴弦的设计，用于其在飞行时发出独特的声音。风筝可以分为两类：大风筝和小风筝。如今，你会看到人们带着孩子在很多公园里放小风筝，还可以看到成年人放更大的风筝，并使用更先进的方法与更粗的绳索，以拽住大型风筝。

古代风筝结构

风筝由三部分组成：框架、胶着和装饰。在框架中，竹子等浅色木材常被用来制作风筝的骨架。这些都很轻，柔韧，却非常结实。许多框架形状很受欢迎，包括鸟类、蝴蝶和龙的传统表现形式，以及无翼的昆虫，如蜈蚣，或神话动物，如龙。

现代风筝结构

现代风筝工匠在传统上进行革新，生产出符合创作者想象力的风筝。塑料和尼龙等材料具有鲜艳的色彩和更强的耐用性。LED 灯和声音特效也增强了风筝的放飞和观看体验感。通过铰链连接风筝的部分结构，使风筝的翼或尾能够运动起来。

Lesson 2　Chinese Kites　风筝

潍坊风筝传统

山东省潍坊市与风筝有着特殊的关系。该市是国际风筝协会的所在地，每年 4 月 20 日至 25 日举办潍坊国际风筝节。风筝爱好者众多，来自世界各地，每年这个时候都来到潍坊参加风筝比赛。游客们蜂拥而至，只是为了观看这个雄伟多彩的奇观。节日的高潮是一年一度的"风筝王"的颁奖仪式。潍坊还有一个专门介绍风筝历史的博物馆。

在华盛顿国家航空航天博物馆的飞行史馆里，一块牌子刻在了中国风筝上，上面说："人类制造的最早的飞机是中国古代的风筝和导弹。"

参考答案

Exercises

Ⅰ. 1—5　d f c h i　　6—10　j b e a g

Ⅱ. 1. the Warring States Period
　　2. wood
　　3. Weifang, Shandong Province
　　4. Lu Ban
　　5. military purposes

Ⅲ. 1. 我陪父母去扫墓以纪念我们的祖先。
　　2. 最初，风筝在战争时期是用于通信的，而不是用来娱乐消遣的。
　　3. 现在，人们把放风筝视为一种娱乐活动，并作为增强体质的一种运动。
　　4. 风筝是由战国时期的哲学家墨子发明的。
　　5. 它由木头制成，用于传递信息。

Ⅳ. Omitted

Lesson 3   Tai Chi   太极

Warm-Up

Work in pairs. Learn the following words and phrases. Then answer the following questions.

1. Can you list some traditional Tai Chi factions?
2. Do you like playing Tai Chi? Why?

➡ Words and Expressions

Read the following words and expressions. Then try to memorize them.

effort *n.* 努力	make great effort 做出很大努力
make an effort 作出努力	laugh at 嘲笑
keep doing sth. 持续做某事	flexibility *n.* 灵活性
flexible *a.* 灵活的；可变动的	stiff *a.* 僵硬的
calm... down 平静下来；镇定下来	

➡ Useful Expressions

1. I am just playing Tai Chi. Would you like to join me?
2. You have to make great effort to practice.
3. Don't laugh at me. I might look funny.
4. It is so difficult to control my body, my legs become sore.
5. It helps develop your strength and flexibility.
6. Let's start all over again.

➡ Dialogue

Watch the animation, then practice the dialogue by reading it aloud with your partner. Read it through at least twice, and change your role each time.

(**Scene:** Sally is a college student in Cultural and Tourism School from China. Sam is an exchange student from America. On campus, Sally is practicing Tai Chi. Sam is very curious

Lesson 3 Tai Chi 太极

about it.)

Sam: Hey, what are you doing?

Sally: I am just playing Tai Chi. Would you like to join me?

Sam: I'd love to, but I know nothing about it, can you teach me?

Sally: Of course, just follow me like this. It seems easy, but it is not as easy as it looks, you have to make great effort to practice.

Sam: Ok, I see. Don't laugh at me. I might look funny.

Sally: Oh, Bend your knees slightly, stretch your arms, move slowly, try to keep your body erect and… no, don't let your body shake, keep your balance.

Sam: It is so difficult to control my body, my legs become sore.

Sally: Keep holding your pose for a while, It helps develop your strength and flexibility.

Sam: I feel my legs are getting stiff. I can't do it any longer.

Sally: You can, you can do it, be patient, Tai Chi is also called "shadow boxing", it will not only calm you down, but also improve your body, and you will learn the best way to conquer others is not by conflict, but by wit.

Sam: You are right! Let's start all over again.

Questions:

1. Is it easy to learn to play Tai Chi?
2. What is Tai Chi also called?
3. What is the benefit to learn to play Tai Chi?

Role-Play

Act it out according to the instructions.

A student from China: Sally

1. To greet Sam and extend welcome to him.
2. Sally tells him what Tai Chi is, and explains the benefit of playing Tai Chi.
3. Sally tells him how to play Tai Chi.

A student from America: Sam

1. To greet Sally.
2. To show curiosity about Tai Chi.
3. To ask how to play Tai Chi.

➡ Passage Reading

Tai Chi was included in China's first list of national intangible cultural heritage in 2006. Tai Chi is based on the traditional Chinese philosophy of Tai Chi, which is one of the most representative philosophical thoughts in ancient China. Tai Chi combines the functions of self-cultivation, physical fitness, and martial arts.

There are many traditional Tai Chi factions, mainly including Chen Shi, Yang Shi, Wu Shi and Sun Shi factions. Although the different factions have something in common, each faction has its own features.

Now Tai Chi is not only prevailing in domestic, but also spreading abroad, becoming one of the most popular bodybuilding exercise in the world.

Useful Words and Expressions:

intangible cultural heritage 非物质文化遗产	philosophy n. 哲学
representative a. 有代表性的	philosophical a. 哲学的
ancient a. 古代的	combine v. 结合
self-cultivation 修身养性	physical fitness 强身健体
martial arts 武术	faction n. 派别
prevail v. 流行	bodybuilding n. 健身

Translation Tasks:

1. 太极拳被列入2006年中国首批国家非物质文化遗产名录。
2. 太极拳是基于中国传统的太极哲学，它是中国古代最具代表性的哲学思想之一。
3. 太极拳兼具修身养性、强身健体和武术的功能。
4. There are many traditional Tai Chi factions, mainly including Chen Shi, Yang Shi, Wu Shi and Sun Shi factions.
5. Although the different factions have something in common, each faction has its own features.
6. Now Tai Chi is not only prevailing in domestic, but also spreading abroad, becoming the most popular bodybuilding exercise in the world.

➡ Exercises

Ⅰ. *Match the following words and phrases, and write the corresponding letter for each item.*

1. philosophy _____ a. 强身健体

2. representative　　_____　　b. 古代的
3. ancient　　_____　　c. 武术
4. combine　　_____　　d. 派别
5. self-cultivation　　_____　　e. 流行
6. physical fitness　　_____　　f. 健身
7. martial arts　　_____　　g. 哲学
8. faction　　_____　　h. 有代表性的
9. prevail　　_____　　i. 结合
10. bodybuilding　　_____　　j. 修身养性

Ⅱ. *Fill in the blanks according to the text.*

1. Bend your knees slightly, stretch your arms, move slowly, try to keep your body erect and… no, don't let your body shake, keep your _____.
2. It is so difficult to control my body, my legs become _____.
3. Keep holding your _____ for a while, It helps develop your strength and flexibility.
4. I feel my legs are getting _____. I can't do it any longer.
5. Tai Chi is also called _____.

Ⅲ. *Translate the following sentences according to the dialogue.*

1. I am just playing Tai Chi. Would you like to join me?
2. I'd love to, but I know nothing about it, can you teach me?
3. Of course, just follow me like this.
4. Don't laugh at me. I might look funny.
5. You will learn the best way to conquer others is not by conflict, but by wit.

Ⅳ. *Work in pairs and discuss the following questions.*

1. What do you think of Tai Chi?
2. What are the different Tai Chi factions?

Knowledge Expansion

The word "Tai Chi" is an ancient Daoist philosophical term symbolizing the interaction of yin and yang, which are opposite manifestations of the same forces in nature. The dynamic interaction of yin and yang, underlying the relation and changing nature of all things, is epitomized in the famous "Tai Chi Diagram".

It is helpful to think of yin and yang as complementary opposites—each fundamentally relies upon, and gives birth to, the other. So, for example, a fundamental theory of Tai Chi is that hardness comes from softness and quickness comes from slowness. In Tai Chi practice emphasis is placed on relaxing the body, and calming and focusing the mind. Tai Chi form movement is performed slowly, accentuating the intention, mechanics, accuracy, and precision of the motion.

The martial arts of China are typically categorized as either "internal" or "external". Tai Chi downplays brute strength and natural ability and emphasizes learned motor skills, nurturing, and the accumulation of hardness through softness, and thus it is considered an internal martial art. In the classical literature, Tai Chi is referred to as the "science of power".

While Tai Chi was originally created as a martial art, it is also, importantly, a holistic art that develops and informs one's life. Physical, mental, and spiritual components are all integral to its practice, and this must be thoroughly understood to grasp the complexity of Taijiquan, to achieve high levels of skill, and to obtain the full benefits of practice.

(Excerpted from www.bing.com)

参考译文

课文阅读

太极拳在2006年被列入中国首批国家非物质文化遗产名录。太极拳以中国传统的太极哲学为基础，太极是古代中国最具代表性的哲学思想之一。太极拳结合了修身养性、强身健体和武术的功能。

太极拳的传统派系很多，主要包括陈氏、杨氏、武氏和孙氏等各派。尽管不同的派系有共同点，但是每个派系都有自己的特征。

现在太极拳不仅在国内盛行，而且在国外传播，成为世界上最受欢迎的健身运动之一。

扩展阅读

太极一词是古老的道家哲学术语，象征着阴和阳的相互作用，这是自然界中相同力量的相反表现。阴阳之间的动态相互作用，是万物之间的关系和不断变化的本质，体现在著名的"太极图"中。

将阴和阳视为互补的对立是很有帮助的——两者在根本上都依赖于彼此，此生而彼生。因此，举例来说，太极拳的基本理论是硬来自于软，快来自于慢。在太极拳练习中，重点放在放松身体、镇定和集中精神上。太极拳的动作缓慢，强调动作的意图、力道、准确性和精确度。

中国的武术通常分为"内部"或"外部"。太极拳淡化了蛮力和自然能力，强调学习运动技能，通过柔软积累硬度，因此被认为是内部武术。在古典文学中，太极拳被称为

"力量科学"。

　　太极拳最初是作为武术创造的，但重要的是，它也是发展和丰富人的生命的整体艺术。身体的、思想的和精神的组成部分都是其练习不可或缺的，必须深刻理解这一点，以掌握太极拳的精髓，掌握高水平的技能并从练习中受益。

参考答案

Exercises

Ⅰ. 1—5　g h b i j　　6—10　a c d e f

Ⅱ. 1. balance
   2. sore
   3. pose
   4. stiff
   5. shadow boxing

Ⅲ. 1. 我正在练习太极拳。你想加入我吗？
   2. 我很乐意，但是对此我一无所知，你能教我吗？
   3. 当然，像这样跟着我练。
   4. 不要嘲笑我。我可能看起来很搞笑。
   5. 你会明白征服他人的最佳方法不是靠冲突，而是靠智慧。

Ⅳ. Omitted

参考文献

[1] 陈光磊. 语言教学中的文化导入 [J]. 语言教学与研究, 1992 (3): 19-30.

[2] 程裕祯. 中国文化要略 [M]. 北京: 外语教育与研究出版社, 2011.

[3] 关世杰. 跨文化交流学 [M]. 北京: 北京大学出版社, 1995.

[4] 胡文仲. 论跨文化交际的实证研究 [J]. 外语教学与研究, 2005 (5): 323-327.

[5] 贾玉新. 跨文化交际学 [M]. 上海: 上海外语教育出版社, 1997.

[6] 梁漱溟. 中国文化要义 [M]. 上海: 上海人民出版社, 2005.

[7] 叶朗, 朱良志. 中国文化读本 [M]. 北京: 外语教学与研究出版社, 2008.

[8] 王力, 中国古代文化常识 [M]. 北京: 北京联合出版公司, 2014.

[9] 张占一. 试议交际文化和知识文化 [J]. 语言教学与研究, 1990 (3): 15-32.

[10] Agar, M. Language Shock: Understanding the Culture of Conversation [M]. New York: Harper Collins Publishers, 1994.

[11] Bennett M Basic Concepts of Intercultural Communication: Selected Readings [C]. Yarmouth: Intercultural Press, 1998.

[12] 平卡姆. 中式英语之鉴 [M]. 北京: 外语教学与研究出版社, 2000.